YOUR PERSONAL HOROSCOPE
2018

PISCES

YOUR PERSONAL HOROSCOPE 2018

PISCES

20th February–20th March

igloobooks

igloobooks

Published in 2017
by Igloo Books Ltd
Cottage Farm
Sywell
NN6 0BJ
www.igloobooks.com

Produced for Igloo Books by Foulsham Publishing Ltd, The Old Barrel Store,
Drayman's Lane, Marlow, Bucks SL7 2FF, England

FIR003 0717
2 4 6 8 10 9 7 5 3 1
ISBN: 978-1-78670-883-0

This is an abridged version of material originally published
in Old Moore's Horoscope and Astral Diary.

Cover design by Charles Wood-Penn
Edited by Bobby Newlyn-Jones

Printed and manufactured in China

CONTENTS

CONTENTS

INTRODUCTION

Your Personal Horoscopes have been specifically created to allow you to get the most from astrological patterns and the way they have a bearing on not only your zodiac sign, but nuances within it. Using the diary section of the book you can read about the influences and possibilities of each and every day of the year. It will be possible for you to see when you are likely to be cheerful and happy or those times when your nature is in retreat and you will be more circumspect. The diary will help to give you a feel for the specific 'cycles' of astrology and the way they can subtly change your day-to-day life. For example, when you see the sign ☿, this means that the planet Mercury is retrograde at that time. Retrograde means it appears to be running backwards through the zodiac. Such a happening has a significant effect on communication skills, but this is only one small aspect of how the Personal Horoscope can help you.

With Your Personal Horoscope the story doesn't end with the diary pages. It includes simple ways for you to work out the zodiac sign the Moon occupied at the time of your birth, and what this means for your personality. In addition, if you know the time of day you were born, it is possible to discover your Ascendant, yet another important guide to your personal make-up and potential.

Many readers are interested in relationships and in knowing how well they get on with people of other astrological signs. You might also be interested in the way you appear to very different sorts of individuals. If you are such a person, the section on Venus will be of particular interest. Despite the rapidly changing position of this planet, you can work out your Venus sign, and learn what bearing it will have on your life.

Using Your Personal Horoscope you can travel on one of the most fascinating and rewarding journeys that anyone can take – the journey to a better realisation of self.

THE ESSENCE OF PISCES

Exploring the Personality of Pisces the Fishes

(20TH FEBRUARY – 20TH MARCH)

What's in a sign?

Pisceans are fascinating people – everyone you come across is likely to admit that fact. By nature you are kind, loving, trustful and inclined to work very hard on behalf of the people you love – and perhaps even those you don't like very much. Your nature is sympathetic and you will do anything you can to improve the lot of those you consider to be worse off than yourself. There is a very forgiving side to your temperament and also a strong artistic flair that can find an outlet in any one of a dozen different ways.

It's true you are difficult to know, and there is a very important reason for this. Your nature goes deep, so deep in fact that someone would have to live with you for a lifetime to plumb even a part of its fathomless depths. What the world sees is only ever a small part of the total magic of this most compulsive and fascinating zodiac sign. Much of your latent power and natural magic is constantly kept bottled up, because it is never your desire to manipulate those around you. Rather, you tend to wait in the shadows until opportunities to come into your own present themselves.

In love you are ardent and sincere, though sometimes inclined to choose a partner too readily and too early. There's a dreamy quality to your nature that makes you easy to adore, but which can also cause difficulties if the practical necessities of life take a very definite second place.

The chances are that you love music and picturesque scenery, and you may also exhibit a definite fondness for animals. You prefer to live in the country rather than in the middle of a noisy and smelly town, and tend to keep a reasonably well-ordered household. Your family can easily become your life and you always need a focus for your energies. You are not at all good at feathering your own nest,

9

unless you know that someone else is also going to benefit on the way. A little more selfishness probably would not go amiss on occasions because you are often far too willing to put yourself out wholesale for people who don't respect your sacrifices. Pisceans can be full of raging passions and are some of the most misunderstood people to be found anywhere within the great circle of the zodiac.

Pisces resources

It is the very essence of your zodiac sign that you are probably sitting there and saying to yourself 'Resources? I have no resources'. Of course you are wrong, though it has to be admitted that a glaring self-confidence isn't likely to be listed amongst them. You are, however, a very deep thinker, and this can turn out to be a great advantage and a useful tool when it comes to getting on in life. Because your natural intuition is so strong (some people would call you psychic), you are rarely fooled by the glib words of others. Your own natural tendency to tell the truth can be a distinct advantage and a great help to you when it comes to getting on in life from a practical and financial viewpoint.

Whilst many of the signs of the zodiac tend to respond to life in an impulsive way, you are more likely to weigh up the pros and cons of any given situation very carefully. This means that when you do take action you can achieve much more success – as well as saving a good deal of energy on the way. People tend to confide in you automatically, so you are definitely at an advantage when it comes to knowing what makes your family and friends tick. At work you can labour quietly and confidently, either on your own or in the company of others. Some people would assert that Pisceans are model employees because you really do not know how to give anything less than your best.

Never underestimate the power of your instincts. Under most circumstances you are aware of the possible outcome of any given situation and should react as your inner mind dictates. Following this course inevitably puts you ahead of the game and explains why so quiet a sign can promote so many winners in life. Not that you are particularly competitive. It's much more important for you to be part of a winning team than to be out there collecting the glory for yourself.

You are dependable, kind, loving and peerless in your defence of those you take to. All of these are incredible resources when used in the correct way. Perhaps most important of all is your ability to get others on your side. In this you cannot be matched.

THE ESSENCE OF PISCES

Beneath the surface

Everyone instinctively knows that there is something very important going on beneath the surface of the Piscean mind, though working out exactly what it might be is a different kettle of fish altogether. The fact is that you are very secretive about yourself and tend to give very little away. There are occasions when this tendency can be a saving grace, but others where it is definitely a great disadvantage. What isn't hard to see is your natural sympathy and your desire to help those in trouble. There's no end gain here, it's simply the way you are. Your inspiration to do anything is rarely rooted in what your own prize is likely to be. In your soul you are poetical, deeply romantic and inextricably tied to the forces and cycles of the world that brought you to birth.

Despite your capacity for single-minded concentration in some matters, you are often subject to mental confusion. Rational considerations often take second place to intuitive foresight and even inspiration. Making leaps in logic isn't at all unusual for you and forms part of the way you judge the world and deal with it.

If you really want to get on in life, and to gain the most you can from your interactions with others, you need to be very truthful in your approach. Somehow or other that means finding out what is really going on in your mind and explaining it to those around you. This is never going to be an easy process, partly because of your naturally secretive ways. Actually some astrologers overplay the tendency of Pisces to keep its secrets. A great deal of the time you simply don't think you have anything to say that would interest others and you always lack confidence in your own judgements. This is a shame because you rarely proceed without thinking carefully and don't often make glaring mistakes.

Many Pisceans develop an ingrained tendency to believe themselves inadequate in some way. Once again this is something you should fight against. Knowing others better, and allowing them to get to know you, might cause you to feel less quirky or strange. Whether you realise it or not you have a natural magnetism that draws others towards you. Try to spend rather less time thinking – though without losing that Piscean ability to meditate which is central to your well-being. If you allow the fascinating world of the Piscean mind to be shared by the people you come to trust, you should become more understandable to people who really want to like you even more.

11

Making the best of yourself

It must be remembered that the zodiac sign of Pisces represents two Fishes, tethered by a cord but constantly trying to break away from each other. This says a great deal about the basic Piscean nature. The inward, contemplative side of your personality is often at odds with the more gregarious and chatty qualities you also possess. Learning about this duality of nature can go at least part of the way towards dealing with it.

Although you often exhibit a distinct lack of self-confidence in your dealings with the world at large, you are, at heart, quite adept, flexible and able to cope under almost any circumstance. All that is really required in order to have a positive influence on life and to be successful is for you to realise what you are capable of achieving. Alas this isn't quite as easy as it might appear, because the introspective depths of your nature make you think too much and cause you to avoid the very actions that would get you noticed more. This can be something of a dilemma for Pisces, though it is certainly not insurmountable.

Never be afraid to allow your sensitivity to show. It is one of your greatest assets and it is part of the reason why other people love you so much – far more, in fact, than you probably realise. Your natural warmth, grace and charm are certain to turn heads on those occasions when you can't avoid being watched. The creative qualities that you possess make it possible for you to manufacture harmonious surroundings, both for yourself and for your family, who are very important to you. At the same time you recognise the practical in life and don't mind getting your hands dirty, especially when it comes to helping someone else out of a mess.

One of the best ruses Pisceans can use in order to get over the innate shyness that often attends the sign is to put on an act. Pisceans are very good natural actors and can easily assume the role of another individual. So, in your dealings with the world at large, manufacture a more confident individual, though without leaving out all the wonderful things that make you what you are now. Play this part for all you are worth and you will then truly be making the best of yourself.

The impressions you give

There is absolutely no doubt that you are more popular, admired and even fancied than you could ever believe. Such is the natural modesty of your zodiac sign that you invariably fail to pick up on those little messages coming across from other people that say 'I think you are wonderful'. If we don't believe in ourselves it's difficult for us to accept that others think we are worth their consideration. Failing to realise your worth to the world at large is likely to be your greatest fault and needs to be corrected.

In a way it doesn't matter, when seen from the perspective of others. What they observe is a warm-hearted individual. Your magnetic personality is always on display, whether you intend it to be or not, which is another reason why you tend to attract far more attention than you would sometimes elicit. Most Pisceans are quite sexy, another quality that is bound to come across to the people you meet, at least some of whom would be willing to jump through hoops if you were to command it.

In short, what you show, and what you think you are, could be two entirely different things. If you don't believe this to be the case you need to carry out a straw poll amongst some of the people you know. Ask them to write down all your qualities as they see them. The result will almost certainly surprise you and demonstrate that you are far more capable, and loveable, than you believe yourself to be. Armed with this knowledge you can walk forward in life with more confidence and feel as content inside as you appear to be when viewed by the world at large.

People rely heavily on you. That much at least you will have noticed in a day-to-day sense. They do so because they know how well you deal with almost any situation. Even in a crisis you show your true colours and that's part of the reason why so many Piscean people find themselves involved in the medical profession. You are viewed as being stronger than you believe yourself to be, which is why everyone tends to be so surprised when they discover that you are vulnerable and inclined to worry.

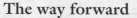

The way forward

You have a great deal to offer the world, even if you don't always appreciate how much. Although you are capable of being shy and introverted on occasions, you are equally likely to be friendly, chatty and very co-operative. You settle to just about any task, though you do possess a sense of freedom that makes it difficult for you to be cooped up in the same place for days and weeks at a stretch. You prefer the sort of tasks that allow your own natural proclivities to shine out, and you exhibit an instinctive creative tendency in almost anything you do.

Use your natural popularity to the full. People are always willing to put themselves out on your behalf, mainly because they know how generous you are and want to repay you for some previous favour. You should never be too proud to accept this sort of proffered help and must avoid running away with the idea that you are unequal to any reasonable task that you set yourself.

It's true that some of your thoughts are extremely deep and that you can get yourself into something of a brown study on occasions, which can be translated by the world around you as depression. However, you are far more stable than you probably believe yourself to be because Pisces is actually one of the toughest of the zodiac signs.

Because you are born of a Water sign it is likely that you would take great delight in living near the sea, or some other large body of water. This isn't essential to your well-being but it does feed your imagination. The vastness of nature in all its forms probably appeals to you in any case and most Pisceans love the natural world with its staggering diversity.

In love you are ardent and sincere, but you do need to make sure that you choose the right individual to suit you. Pisceans often settle for a protecting arm, but if this turns out to be stifling, trouble could follow. You would find it hard to live with anyone who didn't have at least a degree of your sensitivity, and you need a partner who will allow you to retain that sense of inner freedom that is so vital to your well-being.

Make the most of the many gifts and virtues that nature has bestowed upon you and don't be afraid to let people know what you really are. Actually establishing this in the first place isn't easy for you. Pisceans respond well to almost any form of meditation, which is not surprising because the sign of the Fishes is the most spiritually motivated zodiac sign of them all. When you know yourself fully you generate a personality that is an inspiration to everyone.

PISCES ON THE CUSP

Astrological profiles are altered for those people born at either the beginning or the end of a zodiac sign, or, more properly, on the cusps of a sign. In the case of Pisces this would be on the 20th of February and for two or three days after, and similarly at the end of the sign, probably from the 18th to the 20th of March.

The Aquarius Cusp – February 20th to 22nd

This tends to be a generally happy combination of signs, even if some of the people you come into contact with find you rather difficult to understand from time to time. You are quite capable of cutting a dash, as any Aquarian would be, and yet at the same time you have the quiet and contemplative qualities more typified by Pisces. You tend to be seen as an immensely attractive person, even if you are the last one in the world to accept this fact. People find you to be friendly, very approachable and good company in almost any social or personal setting. It isn't hard for you to get on with others, though since you are not so naturally quiet as Pisces when taken alone, you are slightly more willing to speak your mind and to help out, though usually in a very diplomatic manner.

At work you are very capable and many people with this combination find themselves working on behalf of humanity as a whole. Thus work in social services, hospitals or charities really suits the unique combinations thrown up by this sign mixture. Management is right up your street, though there are times when your conception of popularity takes the foremost place in your mind. Occasionally this could take the edge off executive decisions. A careful attention to detail shows you in a position to get things done, even jobs that others shun. You don't really care for getting your hands dirty but will tackle almost any task if you know it to be necessary. Being basically self-sufficient, you also love the company of others, and it is this adaptability that is the hallmark of success to Aquarian-cusp Pisceans.

Few people actually know you as well as they think they do because the waters of your nature run quite deep. Your real task in life is to let the world know how you feel, something you fight shy of doing now and again. There are positive gains in your life, brought about as a result of your adaptable and pleasing nature. Aquarius present in the nature allows Pisces to act at its best.

The Aries Cusp – March 18th to 20th

This is a Piscean with attitude and probably one of the most difficult zodiac sign combinations to be understood, not only by those people with whom you come into contact but clearly by yourself too. If there are any problems thrown up here they come from the fact that Pisces and Aries have such different ways of expressing themselves to the world at large. Aries is very upfront, dynamic and dominant, all factors that are simply diametrically opposed to the way Pisces thinks and behaves. So the real task in life is to find ways to combine the qualities of Pisces and Aries, in a way that suits the needs of both and without becoming totally confused with regard to your basic nature.

The problem is usually solved by a compartmentation of life. For example, many people with this combination will show the Aries qualities strongly at work, whilst dropping into the Piscean mode socially and at home. This may invariably be the case but there are bound to be times when the underlying motivations become mixed, which can confuse those with whom you come into contact.

Having said all of this you can be the least selfish and most successful individual when you are fighting for the rights of others. This is the zodiac combination of the true social reformer, the genuine politician and the committed pacifist. It seems paradoxical to suggest that someone could fight tenaciously for peace, but this is certainly true in your case. You have excellent executive skills and yet retain an ability to tell other people what they should be doing, in fairly strident terms, usually without upsetting anyone. There is a degree of genuine magic about you that makes you very attractive and there is likely to be more than one love affair in your life. A steadfast view of romance may not be naturally present within your basic nature but like so much else you can 'train' this quality into existence.

Personal success is likely, but it probably doesn't matter all that much in a material sense. The important thing to you is being needed by the world at large.

PISCES AND ITS ASCENDANTS

The nature of every individual on the planet is composed of the rich variety of zodiac signs and planetary positions that were present at the time of their birth. Your Sun sign, which in your case is Pisces, is one of the many factors when it comes to assessing the unique person you are. Probably the most important consideration, other than your Sun sign, is to establish the zodiac sign that was rising over the eastern horizon at the time that you were born. This is your Ascending or Rising sign. Most popular astrology fails to take account of the Ascendant, and yet its importance remains with you from the very moment of your birth, through every day of your life. The Ascendant is evident in the way you approach the world, and so, when meeting a person for the first time, it is this astrological influence that you are most likely to notice first. Our Ascending sign essentially represents what we appear to be, while the Sun sign is what we feel inside ourselves.

The Ascendant also has the potential for modifying our overall nature. For example, if you were born at a time of day when Pisces was passing over the eastern horizon (this would be around the time of dawn) then you would be classed as a double Pisces. As such, you would typify this zodiac sign, both internally and in your dealings with others. However, if your Ascendant sign turned out to be a Fire sign, such as Aries, there would be a profound alteration of nature, away from the expected qualities of Pisces.

One of the reasons why popular astrology often ignores the Ascendant is that it has always been rather difficult to establish. We have found a way to make this possible by devising an easy-to-use table, which you will find on page 157 of this book. Using this, you can establish your Ascendant sign at a glance. You will need to know your rough time of birth, then it is simply a case of following the instructions.

For those readers who have no idea of their time of birth it might be worth allowing a good friend, or perhaps your partner, to read through the section that follows this introduction. Someone who deals with you on a regular basis may easily discover your Ascending sign, even though you could have some difficulty establishing it for yourself. A good understanding of this component of your nature is essential if you want to be aware of that 'other person' who is responsible for the way you make contact with the world at large. Your Sun sign, Ascendant sign, and the other pointers in this book will, together, allow you a far better understanding of what makes you tick as an individual. Peeling back the different layers of your astrological make-up can be an enlightening experience, and the Ascendant may represent one of the most important layers of all.

Pisces with Pisces Ascendant

You are a kind and considerate person who would do almost anything to please the people around you. Creative and extremely perceptive, nobody knows the twists and turns of human nature better than you do, and you make it your business to serve humanity in any way you can. Not everyone understands what makes you tick, and part of the reason for this state of affairs is that you are often not really quite 'in' the world as much as the people you encounter in a day-to-day sense. At work you are generally cheerful, though you can be very quiet on occasions, but since you are consistent in this regard, you don't attract adverse attention or accusations of being moody, as some other variants of Pisces sometimes do. Confusion can beset you on occasions, especially when you are trying to reconcile your own opposing needs. There are certain moments of discontent to be encountered which so often come from trying to please others, even when to do so goes against your own instincts.

As age and experience add to your personal armoury you relax more with the world and find yourself constantly sought out for words of wisdom. The vast majority of people care for you deeply.

Pisces with Aries Ascendant

Although not an easy combination to deal with, the Pisces with an Aries Ascendant does bring something very special to the world in the way of natural understanding allied to practical assistance. It's true that you can sometimes be a dreamer, but there is nothing wrong with that as long as you have the ability to turn some of your wishes into reality, and this you are usually able to do, often for the sake of those around you. Conversation comes easily to you, though you also possess a slightly wistful and poetic side to your nature, which is attractive to the many people who call you a friend. A natural entertainer, you bring a sense of the comic to the often serious qualities of Aries, though without losing the determination that typifies the sign.

In relationships you are ardent, sincere and supportive, with a social conscience that sometimes finds you fighting the battles of the less privileged members of society. Family is important to you and this is a combination that invariably leads to parenthood. Away from the cut and thrust of everyday life you relax more fully, and think about matters more deeply than more typical Aries types might.

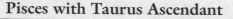

Pisces with Taurus Ascendant

You are clearly a very sensitive type of person and that sometimes makes it rather difficult for others to know how they might best approach you. Private and deep, you are nevertheless socially inclined on many occasions. However, because your nature is bottomless it is possible that some types would actually accuse you of being shallow. How can this come about? Well, it's simple really. The fact is that you rarely show anyone what is going on in the deepest recesses of your mind and so your responses can appear to be trite or even ill-considered. This is far from the truth, as those who are allowed into the 'inner sanctum' would readily admit. You are something of a sensualist, and relish staying in bed late and simply pleasing yourself for days on end. However, you have Taurean traits so you desire a tidy environment in which to live your usually long life.

You are able to deal with the routine aspects of life quite well and can be a capable worker once you are up and firing on all cylinders. It is very important that you maintain an interest in what you are doing, because the recesses of your dreamy mind can sometimes appear to be infinitely more attractive. Your imagination is second to none and this fact can often be turned to your advantage.

Pisces with Gemini Ascendant

There is great duality inherent in this combination, and sometimes this can cause a few problems. Part of the trouble stems from the fact that you often fail to realise what you want from life, and you could also be accused of failing to take the time out to think things through carefully enough. You are reactive, and although you have every bit of the natural charm that typifies the sign of Gemini, you are more prone to periods of self-doubt and confusion. However, you should not allow these facts to get you down too much, because you are also genuinely loved and have a tremendous capacity to look after others, a factor which is more important to you than any other. It's true that personal relationships can sometimes be a cause of difficulty for you, partly because your constant need to know what makes other people tick could drive them up the wall. Accepting people at face value seems to be the best key to happiness of a personal sort, and there are occasions when your very real and natural intuition has to be put on hold.

It's likely that you are an original, particularly in the way you dress. An early rebellious stage often gives way to a more comfortable form of eccentricity. When you are at your best, just about everyone adores you.

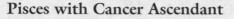

Pisces with Cancer Ascendant

A deep, double Water-sign combination this, and it might serve to make you a very misunderstood, though undoubtedly popular, individual. You are anxious to make a good impression, probably too keen under certain circumstances, and you do everything you can to help others, even if you don't know them very well. It's true that you are deeply sensitive and quite easily brought to tears by the suffering of this most imperfect world that we inhabit. Fatigue can be a problem, though this is somewhat nullified by the fact that you can withdraw completely into the deep recesses of your own mind when it becomes necessary to do so.

You may not be the most gregarious person in the world, simply because it isn't easy for you to put some of your most important considerations into words. This is easier when you are in the company of people you know and trust, though even trust is a commodity that is difficult for you to find, particularly since you may have been hurt by being too willing to share your thoughts early in life. With age comes wisdom and maturity, and the older you are, the better you will learn to handle this potent and demanding combination. You will never go short of either friends or would-be lovers, and may be one of the most magnetic types of both Cancer and Pisces.

Pisces with Leo Ascendant

You are a very sensitive soul, on occasions too much so for your own good. However, there is not a better advocate for the rights of humanity than you represent and you constantly do what you can to support the downtrodden and oppressed. Good causes are your thing and there are likely to be many in your life. You will probably find yourself pushed to the front of almost any enterprise of which you are a part because, despite the deeper qualities of Pisces, you are a natural leader. Even on those occasions when it feels as though you lack confidence, you manage to muddle through somehow and your smile is as broad as the day. Few sign combinations are more loved than this one, mainly because you do not have a malicious bone in your body, and will readily forgive and forget, which the Lion on its own often will not.

Although you are capable of acting on impulse, you do so from a deep sense of moral conviction, so that most of your endeavours are designed to suit other people too. They recognise this fact and will push much support back in your direction. Even when you come across troubles in your life you manage to find ways to sort them out, and will invariably notice something new to smile about on the way. Your sensitivity rating is massive and you can easily be moved to tears.

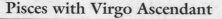

Pisces with Virgo Ascendant

You might have been accused on occasions of being too sensitive for your own good, a charge that is not entirely without foundation. Certainly you are very understanding of the needs of others, sometimes to the extent that you put everything aside to help them. This would also be true in the case of charities, for you care very much about the world and the people who cling tenaciously to its surface. Your ability to love on a one-to-one basis knows no bounds, though you may not discriminate as much as you could, particularly when young, and might have one or two false starts in the love stakes. You don't always choose to verbalise your thoughts and this can cause problems, because there is always so much going on in your mind and Virgo especially needs good powers of communication. Pisces is quieter and you need to force yourself to say what you think when the explanation is important.

You would never betray a confidence and sometimes take on rather more for the sake of your friends than is strictly good for you. This is not a fault but can cause you problems all the same. Because you are so intuitive there is little that escapes your attention, though you should avoid being pessimistic about your insights. Changes of scenery suit you and travel would bring out the best in what can be a repressed nature.

Pisces with Libra Ascendant

An Air and Water combination, you are not easy to understand and have depths that show at times, surprising those people who thought they already knew what you were. You will always keep people guessing and are just as likely to hitchhike around Europe as you are to hold down a steady job, both of which you would undertake with the same degree of commitment and success. Usually young at heart, but always carrying the potential for an old head on young shoulders, you are something of a paradox and not at all easy for totally 'straight' types to understand. But you always make an impression, and tend to be very attractive to members of the opposite sex.

In matters of health you do have to be a little careful because you dissipate much nervous energy and can sometimes be inclined to push yourself too hard, at least in a mental sense. Frequent periods of rest and meditation will do you the world of good and should improve your level of wisdom, which tends to be fairly high already. Much of your effort in life is expounded on behalf of humanity as a whole, for you care deeply, love totally and always give of your best. Whatever your faults and failings might be, you are one of the most popular people around.

Pisces with Scorpio Ascendant

You stand a chance of disappearing so deep into yourself that other people would need one of those long ladders that cave explorers use to even find you. It isn't really your fault, because both Scorpio and Pisces, as Water signs, are difficult to understand and you have them both. But that doesn't mean that you should be content to remain in the dark, and the warmth of your nature is all you need to shine a light on the wonderful qualities you possess. But the primary word of warning is that you must put yourself on display and allow others to know what you are, before their appreciation of these facts becomes apparent.

As a server of the world you are second to none and it is hard to find a person with this combination who is not, in some way, looking out for the people around them. Immensely attractive to others, you are also one of the most sought-after lovers. Much of this has to do with your deep and abiding charm, but the air of mystery that surrounds you also helps. Some of you will marry too early, and end up regretting the fact, though the majority of people with Scorpio and Pisces will find the love they deserve in the end. You are able, just, firm but fair, though a sucker for a hard luck story and as kind as the day is long. It's hard to imagine how so many good points could be ignored by others.

Pisces with Sagittarius Ascendant

A very attractive combination this, because the more dominant qualities of the Archer are somehow mellowed-out by the caring Water-sign qualities of the Fishes. You can be very outgoing, but there is always a deeper side to your nature that allows others to know that you are thinking about them. Few people could fall out with either your basic nature or your attitude to the world at large, even though there are depths to your nature that may not be easily understood. You are capable, have a good executive ability and can work hard to achieve your objectives, even if you get a little disillusioned on the way. Much of your life is given over to helping those around you and there is a great tendency for you to work for and on behalf of humanity as a whole. A sense of community is brought to most of what you do and you enjoy co-operation. Although you have the natural ability to attract people to you, the Pisces half of your nature makes you just a little more reserved in personal matters than might otherwise be the case. More careful in your choices than either sign taken alone, you still have to make certain that your motivations when commencing a personal relationship are the right ones. You love to be happy, and to offer gifts of happiness to others.

Pisces with Capricorn Ascendant

You are certainly not the easiest person in the world to understand, mainly because your nature is so deep and your personality so complicated, that others are somewhat intimidated at the prospect of staring into this abyss. All the same your friendly nature is attractive, and there will always be people around who are fascinated by the sheer magnetic quality that is intrinsic to this zodiac mix. Sentimental and extremely kind, there is no limit to the extent of your efforts on behalf of a deserving world, though there are some people around who wonder at your commitment and who may ridicule you a little for your staying-power, even in the face of some adversity. At work you are very capable, will work long and hard, and can definitely expect a greater degree of financial and practical success than Pisces when taken alone. Routines don't bother you too much, though you do need regular periods of introspection, which help to recharge low batteries and a battered self-esteem. In affairs of the heart you are given to impulse, which belies the more careful qualities of Capricorn. However, the determination remains intact and you are quite capable of chasing rainbows round and round the same field, never realising that you can't get to the end of them. Generally speaking you are an immensely lovable person and a great favourite to many.

Pisces with Aquarius Ascendant

Here we find the originality of Aquarius balanced by the very sensitive qualities of Pisces, and it makes for a very interesting combination. When it comes to understanding other people you are second to none, but it's certain that you are more instinctive than either Pisces or Aquarius when taken alone. You are better at routines than Aquarius, but also relish a challenge more than the typical Piscean would. Active and enterprising, you tend to know what you want from life, but consideration of others, and the world at large, will always be part of the scenario. People with this combination often work on behalf of humanity and are to be found in social work, the medical profession and religious institutions. As far as beliefs are concerned you don't conform to established patterns, and yet may get closer to the truth of the Creator than many deep theological thinkers have ever been able to do. Acting on impulse as much as you do means that not everyone understands the way your mind works, but your popularity will invariably see you through.

Passionate and deeply sensitive, you are able to negotiate the twists and turns of a romantic life that is hardly likely to be run-of-the-mill. In the end, however, you should certainly be able to find a very deep personal and spiritual happiness.

THE MOON AND THE PART IT PLAYS IN YOUR LIFE

In astrology the Moon is probably the single most important heavenly body after the Sun. Its unique position, as partner to the Earth on its journey around the solar system, means that the Moon appears to pass through the signs of the zodiac extremely quickly. The zodiac position of the Moon at the time of your birth plays a great part in personal character and is especially significant in the build-up of your emotional nature.

Your Own Moon Sign

Discovering the position of the Moon at the time of your birth has always been notoriously difficult because tracking the complex zodiac positions of the Moon is not easy. This process has been reduced to three simple stages with our Lunar Tables. A breakdown of the Moon's zodiac positions can be found from page 35 onwards, so that once you know what your Moon Sign is, you can see what part this plays in the overall build-up of your personal character.

If you follow the instructions on the next page you will soon be able to work out exactly what zodiac sign the Moon occupied on the day that you were born and you can then go on to compare the reading for this position with those of your Sun sign and your Ascendant. It is partly the comparison between these three important positions that goes towards making you the unique individual you are.

HOW TO DISCOVER YOUR MOON SIGN

This is a three-stage process. You may need a pen and a piece of paper but if you follow the instructions below the process should only take a minute or so.

STAGE 1 First of all you need to know the Moon Age at the time of your birth. If you look at Moon Table 1, on page 33, you will find all the years between 1920 and 2018 down the left side. Find the year of your birth and then trace across to the right to the month of your birth. Where the two intersect you will find a number. This is the date of the New Moon in the month that you were born. You now need to count forward the number of days between the New Moon and your own birthday. For example, if the New Moon in the month of your birth was shown as being the 6th and you were born on the 20th, your Moon Age Day would be 14. If the New Moon in the month of your birth came after your birthday, you need to count forward from the New Moon in the previous month. If you were born in a Leap Year, remember to count the 29th February. You can tell if your birth year was a Leap Year if the last two digits can be divided by four. Whatever the result, jot this number down so that you do not forget it.

STAGE 2 Take a look at Moon Table 2 on page 34. Down the left hand column look for the date of your birth. Now trace across to the month of your birth. Where the two meet you will find a letter. Copy this letter down alongside your Moon Age Day.

STAGE 3 Moon Table 3 on page 34 will supply you with the zodiac sign the Moon occupied on the day of your birth. Look for your Moon Age Day down the left hand column and then for the letter you found in Stage 2. Where the two converge you will find a zodiac sign and this is the sign occupied by the Moon on the day that you were born.

Your Zodiac Moon Sign Explained

You will find a profile of all zodiac Moon Signs on pages 35 to 38, showing in yet another way how astrology helps to make you into the individual that you are. In each daily entry of the Astral Diary you can find the zodiac position of the Moon for every day of the year. This also allows you to discover your lunar birthdays. Since the Moon passes through all the signs of the zodiac in about a month, you can expect something like twelve lunar birthdays each year. At these times you are likely to be emotionally steady and able to make the sort of decisions that have real, lasting value.

MOON TABLE 1

YEAR	JAN	FEB	MAR	YEAR	JAN	FEB	MAR	YEAR	JAN	FEB	MAR
1920	21	19	20	1953	15	14	15	1986	10	9	10
1921	9	8	9	1954	5	3	5	1987	29	28	29
1922	27	26	28	1955	24	22	24	1988	18	17	18
1923	17	15	17	1956	13	11	12	1989	7	6	7
1924	6	5	5	1957	1/30–		1/31	1990	26	25	26
1925	24	23	24	1958	19	18	20	1991	15	14	15
1926	14	12	14	1959	9	7	9	1992	4	3	4
1927	3	2	3	1960	27	26	27	1993	24	22	24
1928	21	19	21	1961	16	15	16	1994	11	10	12
1929	11	9	11	1962	6	5	6	1995	1/31	29	30
1930	29	28	30	1963	25	23	25	1996	19	18	19
1931	18	17	19	1964	14	13	14	1997	9	7	9
1932	7	6	7	1965	3	1	2	1998	27	26	27
1933	25	24	26	1966	21	19	21	1999	16	15	16
1934	15	14	15	1967	10	9	10	2000	6	4	6
1935	5	3	5	1968	29	28	29	2001	24	23	25
1936	24	22	23	1969	19	17	18	2002	13	12	13
1937	12	11	12	1970	7	6	7	2003	3	1	2
1938	1/31–		2/31	1971	26	25	26	2004	21	20	21
1939	20	19	20	1972	15	14	15	2005	10	9	10
1940	9	8	9	1973	5	4	5	2006	29	28	29
1941	27	26	27	1974	24	22	24	2007	18	16	18
1942	16	15	16	1975	12	11	12	2008	8	6	7
1943	6	4	6	1976	1/31	29	30	2009	26	25	26
1944	25	24	24	1977	19	18	19	2010	15	14	15
1945	14	12	14	1978	9	7	9	2011	4	3	5
1946	3	2	3	1979	27	26	27	2012	23	22	22
1947	21	19	21	1980	16	15	16	2013	12	10	12
1948	11	9	11	1981	6	4	6	2014	1/31	–	1
1949	29	27	29	1982	25	23	24	2015	19	20	19
1950	18	16	18	1983	14	13	14	2016	9	8	8
1951	7	6	7	1984	3	1	2	2017	27	25	27
1952	26	25	25	1985	21	19	21	2018	16	15	17

TABLE 2   MOON TABLE 3

DAY	FEB	MAR		M/D	D	E	F	G	H	I	J
1	D	F		0	AQ	PI	PI	PI	AR	AR	AR
2	D	G		1	PI	PI	PI	AR	AR	AR	TA
3	D	G		2	PI	PI	AR	AR	AR	TA	TA
4	D	G		3	PI	AR	AR	AR	TA	TA	TA
5	D	G		4	AR	AR	AR	TA	TA	GE	GE
6	D	G		5	AR	TA	TA	TA	GE	GE	GE
7	D	G		6	TA	TA	TA	GE	GE	GE	CA
8	D	G		7	TA	TA	GE	GE	GE	CA	CA
9	D	G		8	TA	GE	GE	GE	CA	CA	CA
10	E	G		9	GE	GE	CA	CA	CA	CA	LE
11	E	G		10	GE	CA	CA	CA	LE	LE	LE
12	E	H		11	CA	CA	CA	LE	LE	LE	VI
13	E	H		12	CA	CA	LE	LE	LE	VI	VI
14	E	H		13	LE	LE	LE	LE	VI	VI	VI
15	E	H		14	LE	LE	VI	VI	VI	LI	LI
16	E	H		15	LE	VI	VI	VI	LI	LI	LI
17	E	H		16	VI	VI	VI	LI	LI	LI	SC
18	E	H		17	VI	VI	LI	LI	LI	SC	SC
19	E	H		18	VI	LI	LI	LI	SC	SC	SC
20	F	H		19	LI	LI	LI	SC	SC	SC	SA
21	F	H		20	LI	SC	SC	SC	SA	SA	SA
22	F	I		21	SC	SC	SC	SA	SA	SA	CP
23	F	I		22	SC	SC	SA	SA	SA	CP	CP
24	F	I		23	SC	SA	SA	SA	CP	CP	CP
25	F	I		24	SA	SA	SA	CP	CP	CP	AQ
26	F	I		25	SA	CP	CP	CP	AQ	AQ	AQ
27	F	I		26	CP	CP	CP	AQ	AQ	AQ	PI
28	F	I		27	CP	AQ	AQ	AQ	AQ	PI	PI
29	F	I		28	AQ	AQ	AQ	AQ	PI	PI	PI
30	–	I		29	AQ	AQ	AQ	PI	PI	PI	AR
31	–	I									

AR = Aries, TA = Taurus, GE = Gemini, CA = Cancer, LE = Leo, VI = Virgo,
LI = Libra, SC = Scorpio, SA = Sagittarius, CP = Capricorn, AQ = Aquarius, PI = Pisces

MOON SIGNS

Moon in Aries

You have a strong imagination, courage, determination and a desire to do things in your own way and forge your own path through life.

Originality is a key attribute; you are seldom stuck for ideas although your mind is changeable and you could take the time to focus on individual tasks. Often quick-tempered, you take orders from few people and live life at a fast pace. Avoid health problems by taking regular time out for rest and relaxation.

Emotionally, it is important that you talk to those you are closest to and work out your true feelings. Once you discover that people are there to help, there is less necessity for you to do everything yourself.

Moon in Taurus

The Moon in Taurus gives you a courteous and friendly manner, which means you are likely to have many friends.

The good things in life mean a lot to you, as Taurus is an Earth sign that delights in experiences which please the senses. Hence you are probably a lover of good food and drink, which may in turn mean you need to keep an eye on the bathroom scales, especially as looking good is also important to you.

Emotionally you are fairly stable and you stick by your own standards. Taureans do not respond well to change. Intuition also plays an important part in your life.

Moon in Gemini

You have a warm-hearted character, sympathetic and eager to help others. At times reserved, you can also be articulate and chatty: this is part of the paradox of Gemini, which always brings duplicity to the nature. You are interested in current affairs, have a good intellect, and are good company and likely to have many friends. Most of your friends have a high opinion of you and would be ready to defend you should the need arise. However, this is usually unnecessary, as you are quite capable of defending yourself in any verbal confrontation.

Travel is important to your inquisitive mind and you find intellectual stimulus in mixing with people from different cultures. You also gain much from reading, writing and the arts but you do need plenty of rest and relaxation in order to avoid fatigue.

Moon in Cancer

The Moon in Cancer at the time of birth is a fortunate position as Cancer is the Moon's natural home. This means that the qualities of compassion and understanding given by the Moon are especially enhanced in your nature, and you are friendly and sociable and cope well with emotional pressures. You cherish home and family life, and happily do the domestic tasks. Your surroundings are important to you and you hate squalor and filth. You are likely to have a love of music and poetry.

Your basic character, although at times changeable like the Moon itself, depends on symmetry. You aim to make your surroundings comfortable and harmonious, for yourself and those close to you.

Moon in Leo

The best qualities of the Moon and Leo come together to make you warm-hearted, fair, ambitious and self-confident. With good organisational abilities, you invariably rise to a position of responsibility in your chosen career. This is fortunate as you don't enjoy being an 'also-ran' and would rather be an important part of a small organisation than a menial in a large one.

You should be lucky in love, and happy, provided you put in the effort to make a comfortable home for yourself and those close to you. It is likely that you will have a love of pleasure, sport, music and literature. Life brings you many rewards, most of them as a direct result of your own efforts, although you may be luckier than average and ready to make the best of any situation.

Moon in Virgo

You are endowed with good mental abilities and a keen receptive memory, but you are never ostentatious or pretentious. Naturally quite reserved, you still have many friends, especially of the opposite sex. Marital relationships must be discussed carefully and worked at so that they remain harmonious, as personal attachments can be a problem if you do not give them your full attention.

Talented and persevering, you possess artistic qualities and are a good homemaker. Earning your honours through genuine merit, you work long and hard towards your objectives but show little pride in your achievements. Many short journeys will be undertaken in your life.

Moon in Libra

With the Moon in Libra you are naturally popular and make friends easily. People like you, probably more than you realise, you bring fun to a party and are a natural diplomat. For all its good points, Libra is not the most stable of astrological signs and, as a result, your emotions can be a little unstable too. Therefore, although the Moon in Libra is said to be good for love and marriage, your Sun sign and Rising sign will have an important effect on your emotional and loving qualities.

You must remember to relate to others in your decision-making. Co-operation is crucial because Libra represents the 'balance' of life that can only be achieved through harmonious relationships. Conformity is not easy for you because Libra, an Air sign, likes its independence.

Moon in Scorpio

Some people might call you pushy. In fact, all you really want to do is to live life to the full and protect yourself and your family from the pressures of life. Take care to avoid giving the impression of being sarcastic or impulsive and use your energies wisely and constructively.

You have great courage and you invariably achieve your goals by force of personality and sheer effort. You are fond of mystery and are good at predicting the outcome of situations and events. Travel experiences can be beneficial to you.

You may experience problems if you do not take time to examine your motives in a relationship, and also if you allow jealousy, always a feature of Scorpio, to cloud your judgement.

Moon in Sagittarius

The Moon in Sagittarius helps to make you a generous individual with humanitarian qualities and a kind heart. Restlessness may be intrinsic as your mind is seldom still. Perhaps because of this, you have a need for change that could lead you to several major moves during your adult life. You are not afraid to stand your ground when you know your judgement is right, you speak directly and have good intuition.

At work you are quick, efficient and versatile and so you make an ideal employee. You need work to be intellectually demanding and do not enjoy tedious routines.

In relationships, you anger quickly if faced with stupidity or deception, though you are just as quick to forgive and forget. Emotionally, there are times when your heart rules your head.

Moon in Capricorn

The Moon in Capricorn makes you popular and likely to come into the public eye in some way. The watery Moon is not entirely comfortable in the Earth sign of Capricorn and this may lead to some difficulties in the early years of life. An initial lack of creative ability and indecision must be overcome before the true qualities of patience and perseverance inherent in Capricorn can show through.

You have good administrative ability and are a capable worker, and if you are careful you can accumulate wealth. But you must be cautious and take professional advice in partnerships, as you are open to deception. You may be interested in social or welfare work, which suit your organisational skills and sympathy for others.

Moon in Aquarius

The Moon in Aquarius makes you an active and agreeable person with a friendly, easy-going nature. Sympathetic to the needs of others, you flourish in a laid-back atmosphere. You are broad-minded, fair and open to suggestion, although sometimes you have an unconventional quality which others can find hard to understand.

You are interested in the strange and curious, and in old articles and places. You enjoy trips to these places and gain much from them. Political, scientific and educational work interests you and you might choose a career in science or technology.

Money-wise, you make gains through innovation and concentration and Lunar Aquarians often tackle more than one job at a time. In love you are kind and honest.

Moon in Pisces

You have a kind, sympathetic nature, somewhat retiring at times, but you always take account of others' feelings and help when you can.

Personal relationships may be problematic, but as life goes on you can learn from your experiences and develop a better understanding of yourself and the world around you.

You have a fondness for travel, appreciate beauty and harmony and hate disorder and strife. You may be fond of literature and would make a good writer or speaker yourself. You have a creative imagination and may come across as an incurable romantic. You have strong intuition, maybe bordering on a mediumistic quality, which sets you apart from the mass. You may not be rich in cash terms, but your personal gifts are worth more than gold.

PISCES IN LOVE

Discover how compatible in love you are with people from the same and other signs of the zodiac. Five stars equals a match made in heaven!

Pisces meets Pisces

Pisceans are easy-going and get on well with most people, so when two Pisceans get together, harmony is invariably the result. While this isn't the most dynamic relationship, there is mutual understanding, and a desire to please on both sides. Neither partner is likely to be overbearing or selfish. Family responsibilities should be happily shared and home surroundings will be comfortable, but never pretentious. One of the better pairings for the sign of the Fishes. Star rating: *****

Pisces meets Aries

Still waters run deep, and they don't come much deeper than Pisces. Although these signs share the same quadrant of the zodiac, they have little in common. Pisces is a dreamer, a romantic idealist with steady and spiritual goals. Aries needs to be on the move, and has very different ideals. It's hard to see how a relationship could develop but, with patience, there is a chance that things might work out. Pisces needs incentive, and Aries may be the sign to offer it. Star rating: **

Pisces meets Taurus

No problem here, unless both parties come from the quieter side of their respective signs. Most of the time Taurus and Pisces would live comfortably together, offering mutual support and deep regard. Taurus can offer the personal qualities that Pisces craves, whilst Pisces understands and copes with the Bull's slightly stubborn qualities. Taurus is likely to travel in Piscean company, so there is a potential for wide-ranging experiences and variety which is essential. There will be some misunderstandings, mainly because Pisces is so deep, but that won't prevent their enduring happiness. Star rating: ***

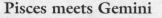

Pisces meets Gemini

Gemini likes to think of itself as intuitive and intellectual, but it will never understand Pisces' dark depths. Another stumbling block is that both Gemini and Pisces are 'split' signs – the Twins and the two Fishes – which means that both are capable of dual personalities. There won't be any shortage of affection, but the real question has to be how much these people feel they have in common. Pisces is extremely kind, and so is Gemini most of the time. But Pisces does too much soul-searching for Gemini, who might eventually become bored. Star rating: ***

Pisces meets Cancer

This is likely to be a very successful match. Cancer and Pisces are both Water signs, both deep, sensitive and very caring. Pisces loves deeply, and Cancer wants to be loved. There will be few fireworks here, and a very quiet house. But that doesn't mean that either love or action is lacking – the latter of which is just behind closed doors. Family and children are important to both signs and both are prepared to work hard, but Pisces is the more restless of the two and needs the support and security that Cancer offers. Star rating: *****

Pisces meets Leo

Pisces always needs to understand others, which makes Leo feel warm and loved, while Leo sees, to its delight, that Pisces needs to be protected and taken care of. Pisceans are often lacking in self-confidence which is something Leo has to spare, and happily it is often infectious. Pisces' inevitable cares are swept away on a tide of Leonine cheerfulness. This couple's home would be cheerful and full of love, which is beneficial to all family members. This is not a meeting of minds, but rather an understanding and appreciation of differences. Star rating: ****

Pisces meets Virgo

This looks an unpromising match from beginning to end. There are exceptions to every rule, particularly where Pisces is concerned, but these two signs are both so deep it's hard to imagine that they could ever find what makes the other tick. The depth is different in each case: Virgo's ruminations are extremely materialistic, while Pisces exists in a world of deep-felt, poorly expressed emotion. Pisces and Virgo might find they don't talk much, so only in a contemplative, almost monastic, match would they ever get on. Still, in a vast zodiac, anything is possible. Star rating: **

Pisces meets Libra

Libra and Pisces can be extremely fond of each other, even deeply in love, but this alone isn't a stable foundation for long-term success. Pisces is extremely deep and doesn't even know itself very well. Libra may initially find this intriguing but will eventually feel frustrated at being unable to understand the Piscean's emotional and personal feelings. Pisces can be jealous and may find Libra's flightiness difficult, which Libra can't stand. They are great friends and they may make it to the romantic stakes, but when they get there a great deal of effort will be necessary. Star rating: ***

Pisces meets Scorpio

If ever there were two zodiac signs that have a total rapport, it has to be Scorpio and Pisces. They share very similar needs: they are not gregarious and are happy with a little silence, good music and time to contemplate the finer things in life, and both are attracted to family life. Apart, they can have a tendency to wander in a romantic sense, but this is reduced when they come together. They are deep, firm friends who enjoy each other's company and this must lead to an excellent chance of success. These people are surely made for each other! Star rating: *****

Pisces meets Sagittarius

Probably the least likely success story for either sign, which is why it scores so low on the star rating. The basic problem is an almost total lack of understanding. A successful relationship needs empathy and progress towards a shared goal but, although both are eager to please, Pisces is too deep and Sagittarius too flighty – they just don't belong on the same planet! As pals, they have more in common and so a friendship is the best hope of success and happiness. Star rating: *

Pisces meets Capricorn

There is some chance of a happy relationship here, but it will need work on both sides. Capricorn is a go-getter, but likes to plan long term. Pisces is naturally more immediate, but has enough intuition to understand the Goat's thinking. Both have patience, but it will usually be Pisces who chooses to play second fiddle. The quiet nature of both signs might be a problem, as someone will have to take the lead, especially in social situations. Both signs should recognise this fact and accommodate it. Star rating: ***

Pisces meets Aquarius

Zodiac signs that follow each other often have something in common, but this is often not the case with Aquarius and Pisces. Both signs are deeply caring, but in different ways. Pisces is one of the deepest zodiac signs, and Aquarius simply isn't prepared to embark on the journey. Pisceans, meanwhile, would probably find Aquarians superficial and even flippant. On the positive side, there is potential for a well-balanced relationship, but unless one party is untypical of their zodiac sign, it often doesn't get started. Star rating: **

VENUS:
THE PLANET OF LOVE

If you look up at the sky around sunset or sunrise you will often see Venus in close attendance to the Sun. It is arguably one of the most beautiful sights of all and there is little wonder that historically it became associated with the goddess of love. But although Venus does play an important part in the way you view love and in the way others see you romantically, this is only one of the spheres of influence that it enjoys in your overall character.

Venus has a part to play in the more cultured side of your life and has much to do with your appreciation of art, literature, music and general creativity. Even the way you look is responsive to the part of the zodiac that Venus occupied at the start of your life, though this fact is also down to your Sun sign and Ascending sign. If, at the time you were born, Venus occupied one of the more gregarious zodiac signs, you will be more likely to wear your heart on your sleeve, as well as to be more attracted to entertainment, social gatherings and good company. If on the other hand Venus occupied a quiet zodiac sign at the time of your birth, you would tend to be more retiring and less willing to shine in public situations.

It's good to know what part the planet Venus plays in your life for it can have a great bearing on the way you appear to the rest of the world and since we all have to mix with others, you can learn to make the very best of what Venus has to offer you.

One of the great complications in the past has always been trying to establish exactly what zodiac position Venus enjoyed when you were born because the planet is notoriously difficult to track. However, we have solved that problem by creating a table that is exclusive to your Sun sign, which you will find on the following page.

Establishing your Venus sign could not be easier. Just look up the year of your birth on the following page and you will see a sign of the zodiac. This was the sign that Venus occupied in the period covered by your sign in that year. If Venus occupied more than one sign during the period, this is indicated by the date on which the sign changed, and the name of the new sign. For instance, if you were born in 1940, Venus was in Aries until the 9th March, after which time it was in Taurus. If you were born before 9th March your Venus sign is Aries, if you were born on or after 9th March, your Venus sign is Taurus. Once you have established the position of Venus at the time of your birth, you can then look in the pages which follow to see how this has a bearing on your life as a whole.

1920 CAPRICORN / 24.2 AQUARIUS /
  19.3 PISCES
1921 ARIES / 8.3 TAURUS
1922 PISCES / 14.3 ARIES
1923 CAPRICORN
1924 ARIES / 10.3 TAURUS
1925 AQUARIUS / 4.3 PISCES
1926 AQUARIUS
1927 PISCES / 26.2 ARIES
1928 CAPRICORN / 23.2 AQUARIUS /
  18.3 PISCES
1929 ARIES / 9.3 TAURUS
1930 PISCES / 13.3 ARIES
1931 CAPRICORN
1932 ARIES / 9.3 TAURUS
1933 AQUARIUS / 4.3 PISCES
1934 AQUARIUS
1935 PISCES / 25.2 ARIES
1936 CAPRICORN / 23.2 AQUARIUS /
  18.3 PISCES
1937 ARIES / 10.3 TAURUS
1938 PISCES / 12.3 ARIES
1939 CAPRICORN
1940 ARIES / 9.3 TAURUS
1941 AQUARIUS / 3.3 PISCES
1942 AQUARIUS
1943 PISCES / 25.2 ARIES
1944 CAPRICORN / 22.2 AQUARIUS /
  18.3 PISCES
1945 ARIES / 11.3 TAURUS
1946 PISCES / 11.3 ARIES
1947 CAPRICORN
1948 ARIES / 8.3 TAURUS
1949 AQUARIUS / 3.3 PISCES
1950 AQUARIUS
1951 PISCES / 24.2 ARIES
1952 CAPRICORN / 22.2 AQUARIUS /
  17.3 PISCES
1953 ARIES
1954 PISCES / 11.3 ARIES
1955 CAPRICORN
1956 ARIES / 8.3 TAURUS
1957 AQUARIUS / 2.3 PISCES
1958 CAPRICORN / 25.2 AQUARIUS
1959 PISCES / 24.2 ARIES
1960 CAPRICORN / 21.2 AQUARIUS /
  17.3 PISCES
1961 ARIES
1962 PISCES / 10.3 ARIES
1963 CAPRICORN
1964 ARIES / 8.3 TAURUS
1965 AQUARIUS / 1.3 PISCES
1966 AQUARIUS
1967 PISCES / 23.2 ARIES

1968 SAGITTARIUS / 26.1 CAPRICORN
1969 ARIES
1970 PISCES / 10.3 ARIES
1971 CAPRICORN
1972 ARIES / 7.3 TAURUS
1973 AQUARIUS / 1.3 PISCES
1974 CAPRICORN / 2.3 AQUARIUS
1975 PISCES / 23.2 ARIES
1976 SAGITTARIUS / 26.1 CAPRICORN
1977 ARIES
1978 PISCES / 9.3 ARIES
1979 CAPRICORN
1980 ARIES / 7.3 TAURUS
1981 AQUARIUS / 28.2 PISCES
1982 CAPRICORN / 4.3 AQUARIUS
1983 PISCES / 23.2 ARIES
1984 SAGITTARIUS / 25.1 CAPRICORN
1985 ARIES
1986 PISCES / 9.3 ARIES
1987 CAPRICORN
1988 ARIES / 7.3 TAURUS
1989 AQUARIUS / 28.2 PISCES
1990 CAPRICORN / 5.3 AQUARIUS
1991 PISCES / 22.2 ARIES /
  20.3 TAURUS
1992 SAGITTARIUS / 25.1 CAPRICORN
1993 ARIES
1994 PISCES / 9.3 ARIES
1995 CAPRICORN
1996 ARIES / 7.3 TAURUS
1997 AQUARIUS / 27.2 PISCES
1998 CAPRICORN / 5.3 AQUARIUS
1999 PISCES / 22.2 ARIES /
  19.3 TAURUS
2000 SAGITTARIUS / 25.1 CAPRICORN
2001 ARIES
2002 PISCES / 9.3 ARIES
2003 CAPRICORN
2004 ARIES / 7.3 TAURUS
2005 AQUARIUS / 27.2 PISCES
2006 CAPRICORN / 5.3 AQUARIUS
2007 PISCES / 22.2 ARIES
2008 SAGITTARIUS / 25.1 CAPRICORN
2009 ARIES
2010 PISCES / 9.3 ARIES
2011 CAPRICORN
2012 ARIES / 7.3 TAURUS
2013 AQUARIUS / 27.2 PISCES
2014 AQUARIUS / 27.2 PISCES
2015 PISCES / 22.2 ARIES
2016 AQUARIUS / 6.2 PISCES
2017 ARIES
2018 PISCES / 9.3 ARIES

VENUS THROUGH THE ZODIAC SIGNS

Venus in Aries

Amongst other things, the position of Venus in Aries indicates a fondness for travel, music and all creative pursuits. Your nature tends to be affectionate and you would try not to create confusion or difficulty for others if it could be avoided. Many people with this planetary position have a great love of the theatre, and mental stimulation is of the greatest importance. Early romantic attachments are common with Venus in Aries, so it is very important to establish a genuine sense of romantic continuity. Early marriage is not recommended, especially if it is based on sympathy. You may give your heart a little too readily on occasions.

Venus in Taurus

You are capable of very deep feelings and your emotions tend to last for a very long time. This makes you a trusting partner and lover, whose constancy is second to none. In life you are precise and careful and always try to do things the right way. Although this means an ordered life, which you are comfortable with, it can also lead you to be rather too fussy for your own good. Despite your pleasant nature, you are very fixed in your opinions and quite able to speak your mind. Others are attracted to you and historical astrologers always quoted this position of Venus as being very fortunate in terms of marriage. However, if you find yourself involved in a failed relationship, it could take you a long time to trust again.

Venus in Gemini

As with all associations related to Gemini, you tend to be quite versatile, anxious for change and intelligent in your dealings with the world at large. You may gain money from more than one source but you are equally good at spending it. There is an inference here that you are a good communicator, via either the written or the spoken word, and you love to be in the company of interesting people. Always on the look-out for culture, you may also be very fond of music, and love to indulge the curious and cultured side of your nature. In romance you tend to have more than one relationship and could find yourself associated with someone who has previously been a friend or even a distant relative.

Venus in Cancer

You often stay close to home because you are very fond of family and enjoy many of your most treasured moments when you are with those you love. Being naturally sympathetic, you will always do anything you can to support those around you, even people you hardly know at all. This charitable side of your nature is your most noticeable trait and is one of the reasons why others are naturally so fond of you. Being receptive and in some cases even psychic, you can see through to the soul of most of those with whom you come into contact. You may not commence too many romantic attachments but when you do give your heart, it tends to be unconditionally.

Venus in Leo

It must become quickly obvious to almost anyone you meet that you are kind, sympathetic and yet determined enough to stand up for anyone or anything that is truly important to you. Bright and sunny, you warm the world with your natural enthusiasm and would rarely do anything to hurt those around you, or at least not intentionally. In romance you are ardent and sincere, though some may find your style just a little overpowering. Gains come through your contacts with other people and this could be especially true with regard to romance, for love and money often come hand in hand for those who were born with Venus in Leo. People claim to understand you, though you are more complex than you seem.

Venus in Virgo

Your nature could well be fairly quiet no matter what your Sun sign might be, though this fact often manifests itself as an inner peace and would not prevent you from being basically sociable. Some delays and even the odd disappointment in love cannot be ruled out with this planetary position, though it's a fact that you will usually find the happiness you look for in the end. Catapulting yourself into romantic entanglements that you know to be rather ill-advised is not sensible, and it would be better to wait before you committed yourself exclusively to any one person. It is the essence of your nature to serve the world at large and through doing so it is possible that you will attract money at some stage in your life.

Venus in Libra

Venus is very comfortable in Libra and bestows upon those people who have this planetary position a particular sort of kindness that is easy to recognise. This is a very good position for all sorts of friendships and also for romantic attachments that usually bring much joy into your life. Few individuals with Venus in Libra would avoid marriage and since you are capable of great depths of love, it is likely that you will find a contented personal life. You like to mix with people of integrity and intelligence but don't take kindly to scruffy surroundings or work that means getting your hands too dirty. Careful speculation, good business dealings and money through marriage all seem fairly likely.

Venus in Scorpio

You are quite open and tend to spend money quite freely, even on those occasions when you don't have very much. Although your intentions are always good, there are times when you get yourself in to the odd scrape and this can be particularly true when it comes to romance, which you may come to late or from a rather unexpected direction. Certainly you have the power to be happy and to make others contented on the way, but you find the odd stumbling block on your journey through life and it could seem that you have to work harder than those around you. As a result of this, you gain a much deeper understanding of the true value of personal happiness than many people ever do, and are likely to achieve true contentment in the end.

Venus in Sagittarius

You are lighthearted, cheerful and always able to see the funny side of any situation. These facts enhance your popularity, which is especially high with members of the opposite sex. You should never have to look too far to find romantic interest in your life, though it is just possible that you might be too willing to commit yourself before you are certain that the person in question is right for you. Part of the problem here extends to other areas of life too. The fact is that you like variety in everything and so can tire of situations that fail to offer it. All the same, if you choose wisely and learn to understand your restless side, then great happiness can be yours.

Venus in Capricorn

The most notable trait that comes from Venus in this position is that it makes you trustworthy and able to take on all sorts of responsibilities in life. People are instinctively fond of you and love you all the more because you are always ready to help those who are in any form of need. Social and business popularity can be yours and there is a magnetic quality to your nature that is particularly attractive in a romantic sense. Anyone who wants a partner for a lover, a spouse and a good friend too would almost certainly look in your direction. Constancy is the hallmark of your nature and unfaithfulness would go right against the grain. You might sometimes be a little too trusting.

Venus in Aquarius

This location of Venus offers a fondness for travel and a desire to try out something new at every possible opportunity. You are extremely easy to get along with and tend to have many friends from varied backgrounds, classes and inclinations. You like to live a distinct sort of life and gain a great deal from moving about, both in a career sense and with regard to your home. It is not out of the question that you could form a romantic attachment to someone who comes from far away or be attracted to a person of a distinctly artistic and original nature. What you cannot stand is jealousy, for you have friends of both sexes and would want to keep things that way.

Venus in Pisces

The first thing people tend to notice about you is your wonderful, warm smile. Being very charitable by nature you will do anything to help others, even if you don't know them well. Much of your life may be spent sorting out situations for other people, but it is very important to feel that you are living for yourself too. In the main, you remain cheerful, and tend to be quite attractive to members of the opposite sex. Where romantic attachments are concerned, you could be drawn to people who are significantly older or younger than yourself or to someone with a unique career or point of view. It might be best for you to avoid marrying whilst you are still very young.

PISCES:
2017 DIARY PAGES

October 2017

1 SUNDAY
Moon Age Day 11   Moon Sign Aquarius

A personal matter is likely to put you on the defensive today but do make sure you are not defending yourself before you have even been attacked. The people who matter the most will be on your side at the moment and are unlikely to let you down, even if the going gets a little difficult.

2 MONDAY
Moon Age Day 12   Moon Sign Aquarius

Refuse to take on any tasks or to start a completely new regime until you are sure in your own mind that present necessities are catered for. You are fairly quiet, because of a twelfth house Moon, and this period allows you to see things in stark contrast, freed from some social obligations.

3 TUESDAY
Moon Age Day 13   Moon Sign Pisces

This is a day of high energy and maximum achievement. Catapulted out of your twelfth house moon lethargy, you now surge forward positively, making for a potentially interesting and eventful period. Confusion of any sort is blown away by a necessary and welcome wind of change.

4 WEDNESDAY
Moon Age Day 14   Moon Sign Pisces

Getting your own way with others ought to be a piece of cake at the moment. With a natural sense of good luck, together with poise, balance and a determination to get on well, very little should be denied to you this Wednesday. The thing to avoid is staying around at home with nothing particular to do.

5 THURSDAY   *Moon Age Day 15   Moon Sign Aries*

This should be a potentially wonderful time in terms of personal relationships. There are quite a few planetary aspects and positions now working in your favour and very little to get in the way of romantic bliss. If you are not involved in a personal attachment right now, perhaps you should be keeping your eyes open.

6 FRIDAY   *Moon Age Day 16   Moon Sign Aries*

If you have to rethink a particular plan of action, don't see the procedure as being necessarily bad. On the contrary, the more you rush into things right now, the greater is the likelihood of making a mistake. People you haven't seen for quite some time could be making a renewed appearance in your life.

7 SATURDAY   *Moon Age Day 17   Moon Sign Taurus*

This may be the best time of this month to have a clear out in your life. It could be that there are certain business or social relationships that have been holding you back or people who simply don't seem to have your best interests at heart. You are far from being hard-hearted but may be forced by circumstances to look hard at situations.

8 SUNDAY   *Moon Age Day 18   Moon Sign Taurus*

Any outdoor pursuits you may follow are especially well highlighted now, as the more sporting and competitive side of your nature also begins to show itself. Because you are feeling somewhat brave at present, you may choose to tackle an issue that has had you quaking in your boots at some stage in the past.

9 MONDAY   *Moon Age Day 19   Moon Sign Taurus*

This may be the time to bring something to a successful conclusion – a possible scenario that has been around for a few days but which looks even more pertinent now. Be on the lookout for ways to improve your life and also your finances. A change of scene would probably be welcome so try to get some time out and about if you can.

10 TUESDAY
Moon Age Day 20   Moon Sign Gemini

It can benefit you greatly to keep in touch with people who are in the know. Because of your generally affable ways, people like you a great deal. Don't be afraid to turn this fact to your advantage and call in some assistance. Moving towards the culmination of plans you hatched some time ago, you should make material progress.

11 WEDNESDAY
Moon Age Day 21   Moon Sign Gemini

With a greater sense of freedom and adventure than you have experienced for some weeks, it looks as though this part of October is turning very much to your advantage. What you find within yourself right now is greater confidence and a definite desire to get on well, both practically and socially.

12 THURSDAY
Moon Age Day 22   Moon Sign Cancer

Your potential for personal freedom is very strong. This can make you something of a loose cannon on occasion because people who think they know you well are likely to be constantly surprised by your actions and reactions. It doesn't do any harm at all to keep the world guessing once in a while.

13 FRIDAY
Moon Age Day 23   Moon Sign Cancer

This is another marvellous period to get out into the world of social interaction and to make certain that your voice is heard. You will be making some new contacts today, most likely people who will become firm friends and who are in a good position to offer you some timely support.

14 SATURDAY
Moon Age Day 24   Moon Sign Leo

Social affairs should be a breeze at the moment. You have exactly what it takes to get on well with the crowd and any shyness that typifies Pisces seems to be taking a holiday for the moment. Don't be in too much of a rush to get a particular job done. It would be best to wait a while and to make sure it is done properly.

15 SUNDAY
Moon Age Day 25   Moon Sign Leo

You might have to let go of something at present if you want to make life less complicated. Perhaps you are too emotionally involved with a person or situation that is proving to be quite a problem? Whatever the difficulty might be, you can gain by putting distance between yourself and it to take some valuable thinking time.

16 MONDAY
Moon Age Day 26   Moon Sign Virgo

This certainly isn't the most progressive day of the month. The lunar low can make you feel sluggish and could see you putting off something you have been planning for a while. Make the day your own by doing exactly what takes your fancy. If that means curling up with a book, then so be it.

17 TUESDAY
Moon Age Day 27   Moon Sign Virgo

Major decisions should be left until later. You are not really in a position to take chances at the moment and might regret the fact if you do. For the moment, simply coast along and watch others setting the pace. You should be able to get a good deal from friendships and pastimes that you always enjoy.

18 WEDNESDAY
Moon Age Day 28   Moon Sign Libra

You now find yourself in a regenerative phase. The Sun is still occupying your solar eighth house, good for new starts of any sort. Active and enterprising, the lunar low has given you the time to recharge your batteries and allows you to now move forward in a very progressive way indeed.

19 THURSDAY
Moon Age Day 29   Moon Sign Libra

There could be good news coming in from far and wide, some of which you should find either exciting or at the very least joyful. Financial gains are possible, even if these seem to come despite your own best efforts and not because of them. Keep in touch with colleagues who can be of specific practical use to you.

20 FRIDAY
Moon Age Day 0   Moon Sign Libra

Much energy now seems to be going into chasing money and success. You need cash, everyone does, but this type of success might be something of an illusion, as Pisces is inclined to realise. What matters most is happiness and there should be a good deal of that around if you are willing to recognise its potential.

21 SATURDAY
Moon Age Day 1   Moon Sign Scorpio

You actively like people and enjoy the contact you have with them. This is apparent today because you will do almost anything to be amongst groups and with individuals you find interesting. What wouldn't be so comfortable for you today would be to find yourself left to your own devices and devoid of company.

22 SUNDAY
Moon Age Day 2   Moon Sign Scorpio

Making any sort of important change is likely to be quite easy today, though you may have to deal with the slightly odd behaviour of a few of the people you need to rely on at this time. Controversy is likely to touch you at some stage during the day, even if you are not the one who it is focused upon.

23 MONDAY
Moon Age Day 3   Moon Sign Sagittarius

You can get a great deal out of journeys of any sort and although the summer is now over, you might decide that the time is right to take a holiday. Travel that is organised at very short notice could be the most enjoyable of all and you can also gain from mixing with people who come from far away.

24 TUESDAY
Moon Age Day 4   Moon Sign Sagittarius

Success right now has a great deal to do with the influence you have over others. You may have to change your mind about something you thought you understood well but you won't lose credibility if you are able to explain yourself. Trends continue to suggest that controversy can dog your footsteps, perhaps in terms of your personal life.

25 WEDNESDAY   *Moon Age Day 5   Moon Sign Sagittarius*

Contact with a variety of different sorts of people really makes life go with a swing and you cannot afford to hide either your nature or your talents at present. If you are good at something, now is the time to show this fact to the world at large. Romance could be on the cards for both young and young-at-heart Pisceans.

26 THURSDAY   *Moon Age Day 6   Moon Sign Capricorn*

A personal plan or a specific intention on your part may now have to be scrapped, probably through no fault of your own. If this leads to some disappointment, the best way forward is to forget about a situation that is in the past and to push even harder for the winning post in other ways. People make a fuss of you later today.

27 FRIDAY   *Moon Age Day 7   Moon Sign Capricorn*

Ideas could fail to turn out quite as you had expected and that could mean being forced to alter your strategy at a moment's notice. This should not present you with too many problems, since your mind is working quickly and you don't have too much trouble thinking on your feet under present astrological trends.

28 SATURDAY   *Moon Age Day 8   Moon Sign Aquarius*

You should let your personality shine out this weekend because there are plenty of people watching you, some of whom are deeply attracted to that Piscean nature of yours. Don't be too modest and when you are asked for your opinion, do your best to act as though you have the right to offer it.

29 SUNDAY   *Moon Age Day 9   Moon Sign Aquarius*

There are planets around now that emphasise your obligations to others, which might be something of a drag during one of those few occasions for Pisces that you are thinking about yourself. It won't be long before a particularly tedious job is out of the way, which should leave you with more time to do as you please.

30 MONDAY
Moon Age Day 10   Moon Sign Pisces

There are some new and tempting ideas around at the moment and you won't be tardy when it comes to accepting an offer you seem to have been waiting for a long time. Your effectiveness at work goes without saying and you might even be able to turn heads when it comes to social situations at present.

31 TUESDAY
Moon Age Day 11   Moon Sign Pisces

This is the time when it helps to put in that extra push that can make all the difference to your situation. Some of your victories are hard won but the fact that you get there in the end is what counts. You have good persuasive powers today and shouldn't give in simply because someone seems to be saying no at first.

November 2017

1 WEDNESDAY   *Moon Age Day 12*   *Moon Sign Pisces*

The start of November marks a good time for some sort of professional accomplishment. Certain matters that have been on hold for a while could well come to fruition now and the chance of making money is quite good. Other trends indicate that friends may have a special need of you around this time.

2 THURSDAY   *Moon Age Day 13*   *Moon Sign Aries*

The social highlights continue, making this a very good time for having fun and for making new friends. There are a number of confidences coming your way right now and it is very important that you guard these carefully since your reputation with some people might rest on your discretion.

3 FRIDAY   *Moon Age Day 14*   *Moon Sign Aries*

This might be a period during which you should be getting as much rest as possible. It isn't that any trends are working against your best interests but simply that you have reached the end of a particular phase and need to take a break before starting on something else. From a personal viewpoint, today should find you very content.

4 SATURDAY   *Moon Age Day 15*   *Moon Sign Taurus*

There are some new and interesting people around at the moment. If you haven't already taken this fact into account, perhaps you should do so today. Whether you meet these people at work or within your home-life, you can get a great deal out of new encounters. These should furnish you with schemes and plans for next year.

5 SUNDAY
Moon Age Day 16   Moon Sign Taurus

You can make today very interesting for yourself but there are likely to be a few small setbacks to take into account. It is possible that in the middle of enjoying yourself, there will be a number of people around who have it in mind to make you work! This really isn't the way you are feeling and even Pisces fights back sometimes.

6 MONDAY
Moon Age Day 17   Moon Sign Gemini

You are out there in the social mainstream today, even if that is not exactly where you planned on being. At every level, work takes something of a back seat, in favour of having fun. Your confidence isn't lacking, especially when you are in the company of people who naturally make you feel good.

7 TUESDAY
Moon Age Day 18   Moon Sign Gemini

It is easier to address the needs and wants of loved ones today, rather than spending too much time thinking about what you want for yourself. This is the truly unselfish quality of Pisces, which is never really very far from the surface. Your intuition works well when you are dealing with strangers.

8 WEDNESDAY
Moon Age Day 19   Moon Sign Cancer

You are in a go-ahead frame of mind but you manifest this slightly differently from usual now. If someone is needed to cheer up the 'grump of the month', then that person is definitely you. Your sense of humour is especially infectious and you have a natural wisdom that hardly anyone could fail to recognise.

9 THURSDAY
Moon Age Day 20   Moon Sign Cancer

This is a good day from a professional point of view and it is easy to make allies at every stage. A continued reliance on a specific individual could lead to one or two problems, especially if the person concerned fails to live up to your expectations. Embark on new projects with as much confidence as you can muster.

10 FRIDAY   *Moon Age Day 21   Moon Sign Leo*

You need to broaden your horizons as much as possible and avoid being in any way restricted in your thinking. Pisces shows itself as being very creative in terms of ideas around now, a factor that can stand you in good stead, both at home and at work. Keep abreast of current affairs as what you learn could be useful for the future.

11 SATURDAY   *Moon Age Day 22   Moon Sign Leo*

The opportunities for overall gain are good, though you could find yourself so keen on breaking down barriers and increasing your personal freedom that you don't address the financial aspect of life at all. Avoid listening to either rumours or gossip, both of which are highly likely to be wrong.

12 SUNDAY   *Moon Age Day 23   Moon Sign Virgo*

Even if you have to change direction in midstream, the fact that life is zipping along nicely is what matters the most. It is possible to see progress being made, though without feeling situations are out of control or that you have to become someone else in order to maintain the pace.

13 MONDAY   *Moon Age Day 24   Moon Sign Virgo*

Contacts with superiors at work might lead to a better understanding of important issues and could even prove advantageous to you personally in the fullness of time. A task to which there seems to have been no end should be drawing to a close before very long, leaving you with more time to do other things.

14 TUESDAY   *Moon Age Day 25   Moon Sign Libra*

It ought to be fairly easy to get your own way in personal relationships at present. All you have to do is turn on the charm and then wait to see the results. Your life is likely to be running fairly smoothly and there could be some interesting possibilities coming your way in a social sense.

15 WEDNESDAY   *Moon Age Day 26   Moon Sign Libra*

Variety is the spice of life, though it has to be said that you are primarily responsible for keeping things on the move at the moment. Trends suggest that an exchange of ideas could be quite illuminating and might cause you to modify your own thinking regarding a fairly important issue.

16 THURSDAY   *Moon Age Day 27   Moon Sign Libra*

Current trends leave you with some new directions in which to travel, either in a real or a figurative sense. Unfortunately, you might not be feeling especially brave at present but you should be able to keep this hidden so that just about everyone you meet thinks you are the bee's knees. Don't be too quick to step aside in favour of someone else.

17 FRIDAY   *Moon Age Day 28   Moon Sign Scorpio*

A significant intellectual boost makes itself felt around this time. Good conversation is something you really enjoy now and over the weekend and you can also have a stronger influence on the actions of your partner or family members than you might have been expecting. There are possible new rewards around most corners.

18 SATURDAY   *Moon Age Day 0   Moon Sign Scorpio*

You will be attending to a number of different jobs today but like the juggler you are it is possible to keep all the balls in the air at the same time. Not everyone believes in you right now but the people who matter the most will and that fact should be enough to see you through one or two potentially sticky moments.

19 SUNDAY   *Moon Age Day 1   Moon Sign Sagittarius*

You should find yourself on the right side of some interesting situations today, even if you have to dream them up for yourself. Not everyone displays the same sort of sense of humour that you do right now but that doesn't matter because you will make people laugh in one way or another. Look after cash in the afternoon and evening.

20 MONDAY   *Moon Age Day 2*   *Moon Sign Sagittarius*

A boost to teamwork and all co-operative ventures comes along at this time and you should make the most of these positive trends. You are getting on well with just about everyone, even if there are one or two awkward types around. Your creative potential is especially good and some of you will be thinking about redecorating.

21 TUESDAY   *Moon Age Day 3*   *Moon Sign Sagittarius*

When it comes to furthering your ambitions you are clearly second to none, even though you might have to enlist the support of others on the way. There are likely to be some unexpected events happening around this time but you should manage to deal with them relatively easily. There could be a new attachment on the way.

22 WEDNESDAY   *Moon Age Day 4*   *Moon Sign Capricorn*

Self-confidence in professional matters is clearly the way forward and you won't get anywhere at all if you fail to show those around you that you know what you are talking about. In social and family situations you are clearly putting everyone ahead of yourself, which isn't exactly unusual for Pisces.

23 THURSDAY   *Moon Age Day 5*   *Moon Sign Capricorn*

Close companions may now cause you to think quite deeply about the importance you have placed upon relationships of late. It is possible that you may decide to spend some of your social hours with people you don't see very often. This would be a good day for sending letters or for making a long-distance telephone call.

24 FRIDAY   *Moon Age Day 6*   *Moon Sign Aquarius*

New life can be breathed into situations you thought were over and done with. It is possible that someone might trust you with an important confidence and it will be of paramount importance that you keep it. Friends are likely to be particularly demanding of your time and that won't leave quite as many hours as you might have wished for practical matters.

25 SATURDAY   *Moon Age Day 7   Moon Sign Aquarius*

You might prove to be far too impetuous regarding the decisions you are making today and do need to think carefully about most matters. Although you might not feel you have the confidence of family members, in all probability they will back you when it really counts. Don't get involved in pointless rows.

26 SUNDAY   *Moon Age Day 8   Moon Sign Aquarius*

Your intuition is now much increased and it would be wise to turn it in the direction of people who are coming new into your life. These might be individuals who you meet on a professional level, or perhaps potential friends for the future. Not everything is what it seems – and it might take you a little while to work out why.

27 MONDAY   *Moon Age Day 9   Moon Sign Pisces*

This is definitely the time to let your light shine. There are gains to be made in just about all the areas of your life and a cheerful attitude on your part that gets you into the good books of people who really count. Personality-wise you are willing to throw caution to the wind, which makes you even more attractive.

28 TUESDAY   *Moon Age Day 10   Moon Sign Pisces*

You should prepare yourself for some heart-warming surprises and for a few gains that you didn't expect. Everyday matters turn up the results you have been expecting and probably more besides. With a positive and useful time ahead, you may decide to start enjoying yourself as much as you can.

29 WEDNESDAY   *Moon Age Day 11   Moon Sign Aries*

You can make an extremely powerful impression on those further up the tree than you are and will want to do everything you can to be noticed at the moment. There is much to be gained by being watched, even if to be so goes against the Piscean grain in one way or another. This would be a great time to take a trip.

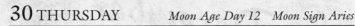

30 THURSDAY
Moon Age Day 12   Moon Sign Aries

Avoid being too pushy at the moment because it probably won't get you very far. You need to display the humility that is part of the basic nature of your zodiac sign and then you will have everyone eating out of your hand. Your confidence grows by the moment when you are doing professional jobs you understand.

December 2017

1 FRIDAY
Moon Age Day 13   Moon Sign Taurus

The things you learn from colleagues today can be of supreme importance, so it is very important to pay attention. Pisces people who are looking for work or a change of employment could also be in luck around this time. When it comes to out-of-work activities, new interests take your fancy.

2 SATURDAY
Moon Age Day 14   Moon Sign Taurus

A sense of variety and freedom is both important and appealing to Pisceans at this time. Don't be a stick-in-the-mud. Although this might not be exactly the season for outdoor activities, you should still find the lure of the wild appealing. Later in the day, you may choose to spend at least some time alone.

3 SUNDAY
☿ *Moon Age Day 15   Moon Sign Gemini*

Although it has occurred to you for some weeks now that Christmas is just around the corner, this is probably the first weekend you have had the chance to do much preparation for it. A shopping spree might be more fun than you would usually expect and you can also rely on the very important help of family members.

4 MONDAY
☿ *Moon Age Day 16   Moon Sign Gemini*

Continuing generally improving trends make themselves felt most in the workplace and in your ability to attract money. Your decision-making is good at present and you can afford to back your hunches to a greater extent. Friends should prove to be quite reliable and there are some new pals in the offing.

5 TUESDAY ☿ *Moon Age Day 17   Moon Sign Cancer*

An excellent day for social occasions and for getting together with the people you care for. Work might have to take something of a back seat because your mind is set firmly on having fun. Routines may be especially annoying so try to get them out of the way as early in the day as possible to make time for more interesting matters later.

6 WEDNESDAY ☿ *Moon Age Day 18   Moon Sign Cancer*

Don't dither or hang back when it comes to making major decisions. The more ambitious you are, the greater is your potential for success. Trends suggest that results you have been seeking for some time will be closer than you think and there is tremendous potential for doing just the right thing when it matters the most.

7 THURSDAY ☿ *Moon Age Day 19   Moon Sign Leo*

The planetary emphasis falls on finances, which might be handy considering this expensive time of year. You are quite canny at the moment and know full well how to get value for money. Even well in advance of the traditional sales, you might be able to search out one or two things for Christmas at rock-bottom prices.

8 FRIDAY ☿ *Moon Age Day 20   Moon Sign Leo*

A fast pace of events in the professional or practical world is probably what you can expect today. There is vital information there for the taking and you won't be slow to pick up on what others are trying to tell you. Give yourself a pat on the back for a recent personal success but don't allow it to go to your head.

9 SATURDAY ☿ *Moon Age Day 21   Moon Sign Virgo*

You now have to put up with the last lunar low of the year, though for a host of astrological reasons you might fail to even register its presence now. You have great momentum and can whizz through difficult moments almost without noticing them. Trends do send a warning, however, to be wary of someone you know and remember that not everyone is trustworthy.

10 SUNDAY ☿ *Moon Age Day 22   Moon Sign Virgo*

The slack pace of progress might annoy you, though there is a good chance that you won't lose too much momentum, or alternatively that it won't bother you at all because you are in a relaxed Sunday mood. There isn't much doubt about the Piscean desire to enjoy itself right now.

11 MONDAY ☿ *Moon Age Day 23   Moon Sign Virgo*

Some of the things that are happening around you at present seem less fulfilling. Tackle this by broadening your horizons and not allowing yourself to be intimidated by little setbacks. The lunar low doesn't really help the situation but whether or not you enjoy what today has on offer seems to be up to you.

12 TUESDAY ☿ *Moon Age Day 24   Moon Sign Libra*

As you grow more and more confident after the lunar low, so you are less intimidated by finding yourself in the limelight. It is true that others will be making a fuss of you at the moment and you are likely to make the most of the situation. Today is also very good for all aspects of romance and one-to-one encounters.

13 WEDNESDAY ☿ *Moon Age Day 25   Moon Sign Libra*

If you try to take on too many diverse interests today this could prove to be a mistake. You would be much better off concentrating on one thing at a time and avoiding unnecessary mistakes. A methodical and steady approach could lead to success, leaving plenty of time in which to enjoy yourself.

14 THURSDAY ☿ *Moon Age Day 26   Moon Sign Scorpio*

This would be a good time to take a short break and to mull over your present successes. You might not be able to see everything in its true light just at the moment but where it matters the most you begin to see a chink of light at the end of the tunnel. Friends will demand your time and you will be happy to help if you can.

15 FRIDAY ☿ *Moon Age Day 27   Moon Sign Scorpio*

The quickening of the pace around you in everyday life is now very obvious and you will barely have time to breathe right now. Don't leave travel plans to chance but make sure that all details are sorted well in advance of any journey you intend to take this week or perhaps during the Christmas break.

16 SATURDAY ☿ *Moon Age Day 28   Moon Sign Scorpio*

A boost to all social matters comes along and it looks as though you are already getting yourself into a Christmas frame of mind. All is happiness around you and if you have been a little restricted by the negative attitude of friends or family members, this sort of situation is now likely to be disappearing.

17 SUNDAY ☿ *Moon Age Day 29   Moon Sign Sagittarius*

Intellectual inspiration comes your way through conversations with people socially, or perhaps through travel. It seems that others find you extremely entertaining to have around and they could be making you feel like a celebrity at the moment. Confidences come in thick and fast, some of them from directions you certainly would not have expected.

18 MONDAY ☿ *Moon Age Day 0   Moon Sign Sagittarius*

Some people might describe you as being too assertive at present but if they do it's probably only because they are used to getting their own way. All that is happening is that you know what you want from life and are presently willing to say so. Avoid getting into pointless discussions about things that don't matter.

19 TUESDAY ☿ *Moon Age Day 1   Moon Sign Capricorn*

This can be an especially rewarding day for many Pisceans, a situation that is brought about as a result of a cocktail of positive planetary positions. You are able to confirm one or two suspicions regarding someone you haven't trusted for a while but in the main you find others to be reliable and helpful.

20 WEDNESDAY ☿ *Moon Age Day 2   Moon Sign Capricorn*

Venus is now in your solar twelfth house and this causes you to reassess the effect you have on those around you. This is likely to be a generally positive process but you are inclined to doubt yourself on occasion and this tendency does show. Stay as positive as you can about all issues that arise today.

21 THURSDAY ☿ *Moon Age Day 3   Moon Sign Capricorn*

It could become quite clear that a change in attitude is necessary when it comes to personal attachments. Maybe your partner is behaving in a slightly odd way and it's up to you to discover why this might be. Getting ahead in any practical sense is not likely today and this could be somewhat frustrating.

22 FRIDAY ☿ *Moon Age Day 4   Moon Sign Aquarius*

Right now you should be enjoying high points in love and romantic affairs, not to mention receiving a definite boost to your ego that comes from a number of different directions. You clearly believe in yourself and while this is the case you won't be short of ideas or ways in which you can make them work out as you would wish.

23 SATURDAY *Moon Age Day 5   Moon Sign Aquarius*

Faces old and new come along now, immediately ahead of the Christmas period. You might be deliberately taking a trip down memory lane at some stage today because that is what Christmas is all about. With only a few days to go, most Pisceans should now be pleased with the arrangements they have made.

24 SUNDAY *Moon Age Day 6   Moon Sign Pisces*

Your potential for lucky breaks is greater than usual on this Christmas Eve and you won't be inclined to look on the negative side of any situation at present. It should be easy to pull in a favour or two and your general level of popularity seems higher than ever. In reality, you are always popular but you realise it more at this time.

25 MONDAY   *Moon Age Day 7   Moon Sign Pisces*

What could be better than a lunar high that coincides with Christmas Day? It makes you bright and breezy and gives you all the energy you could possibly need to get through a busy schedule. If there is time to slump on the sofa after lunch, so much the better but you probably won't feel the need for this whilst in your present mood.

26 TUESDAY   *Moon Age Day 8   Moon Sign Pisces*

Getting into heated debates could be more enjoyable than you might imagine and with the lunar high still present, you are hardly likely to lose. Back your hunches to the hilt and do what you can to make progress your middle name. You can also take time out in order to simply enjoy the day.

27 WEDNESDAY   *Moon Age Day 9   Moon Sign Aries*

This is a time for enjoying the company of others for its own sake. You appear to have no agenda whatsoever today and so this might be an excellent time to simply be yourself. This is a concept that is more understandable to Pisces than any of the other twelve zodiac signs.

28 THURSDAY   *Moon Age Day 10   Moon Sign Aries*

You can capitalise on new opportunities and won't be stuck when it comes to expressing your opinions, no matter who is on the receiving end. Although you might not have too much professional influence at the moment, there are ideas coming into your mind right now that you will act upon after the New Year.

29 FRIDAY   *Moon Age Day 11   Moon Sign Taurus*

Variety is clearly the spice of life and you are likely to have more and more energy, even though the holidays might put a dampener on the sort of progress you want to make. You are torn between personal enjoyment and the ability to make a real impression on life and will have to exercise some true Piscean patience.

30 SATURDAY
Moon Age Day 12   Moon Sign Taurus

This should be a fairly brisk time socially and you will almost certainly notice some of the recent frustrations now disappearing. Your confidence is still strong and you remain willing to suspend some actions until next week. As a result there is more time available to simply enjoy yourself in the company of family and friends.

31 SUNDAY
Moon Age Day 13   Moon Sign Gemini

Don't get too tied up with details because it is clearly the overall picture that is important at present. A job you have been involved with for quite some time could be nearly over but once again you might have to shelve such matters as the end of the year celebrations take over. This ought to be a very enjoyable time.

PISCES:
2018 DIARY PAGES

PISCES:
YOUR YEAR IN BRIEF

It is important to give a great push as soon as you can once the new year is underway. There is plenty for you to do during January and February and most of the cards appear to be stacked in your favour. Get any jobs you don't like out of the way quickly and then spend the rest of the time making progress. People from the past could come back into your life and might bring positive news with them.

The more you feel you are really getting into gear, the greater your comfort is likely to be. March and April offer you chances for movement and an ability to get to grips with issues that have been hanging over you since late last year. Comfort and security may concern you in March, but April is more about travel and new starts. People come thick and fast into your life at this time.

It looks very likely that May and June will bring more of the same for most Pisceans as this is a really a good time of year. Friends and relatives give you all the help you need and even strangers seem to be supportive at this time. June especially has plenty of opportunities for travel, even if you are only going a short distance. Your attitude is perky and everyone loves you.

The high summer finds you at your happiest and this is especially the case during July, which could turn out to be the most eventful and contented month of the year for you. Both July and August offer you the chance to travel and since all opportunities to see new places pleases Pisces no end, you should be in your element. Don't be too critical of others and be willing to accept a different point of view. New starts at work seem highly likely.

September and October could bring into focus the fact that some things you intended to do this year you haven't even started. Now is the time to get on with them. You might also be looking at possible new hobbies and perhaps different ways of keeping fit. Generally happy to be on the move, friends should also be very supportive of you at this time.

As the year draws gradually to its close, November and December have plenty going for them in a social and personal sense. There are gains to be made from getting to know new people and also plenty of incentive to push the bounds of the credible. You should be at your best around the Christmas period. Acting on impulse as a New Year comes into view is perhaps not so advisable, but once New Year's Eve has arrived you can prepare yourself to launch into next year.

January 2018

1 MONDAY
Moon Age Day 14   Moon Sign Gemini

If you confide too much in others today, you run the risk of ending up somewhat disappointed. Trends suggest that not everyone will prove to be either as reliable or as secretive as you would want them to be. All in all, this trend could make you suspicious but your intuition is good and if you listen to it you will know who to trust.

2 TUESDAY
Moon Age Day 15   Moon Sign Cancer

The pace of life is likely to be brisk now and there is no shortage of things you want to get done. Look out for some very positive compliments coming your way. You might not exactly believe them but the fact that they are there at all is inclined to make you feel better about life generally.

3 WEDNESDAY
Moon Age Day 16   Moon Sign Cancer

Although this is not the best day of the month for concentrated work of any sort, if you become something of a grazer today, you can have an interesting time. This means looking at life as a whole and not pushing all your attention in one direction. You may be particularly inclined to read at the moment.

4 THURSDAY
Moon Age Day 17   Moon Sign Leo

You should have plenty of energy today and may decide that an outing or a shopping spree would suit you down to the ground. Spend time with family members or friends and also make the most of time spent with romantic partners. If you have specifically been looking for love, now is the time to focus your attention.

5 FRIDAY
Moon Age Day 18   Moon Sign Leo

You are a sucker today for anyone who has the gift of the gab. That's fine but don't allow yourself to be duped by anyone, simply because they spin a good yarn. The planets' message for you is that this would not be an ideal day for making major purchases or for doing anything that relies on instant decisions instead of rational thought.

6 SATURDAY
Moon Age Day 19   Moon Sign Virgo

This is the first lunar low of the year. This is the time each month during which the Moon occupies your opposite sign of Virgo. You might feel slightly under the weather or simply inclined to spend some time quietly on your own. This is not the best day of the month for taking any kind of risk or chance.

7 SUNDAY
Moon Age Day 20   Moon Sign Virgo

If you find one or two mishaps coming along today, don't panic. Either start again at the beginning or seek the help and advice of someone who is a professional in their field. Don't be in the least surprised if you turn out to be someone's special cup of tea because your popularity is now gradually increasing.

8 MONDAY
Moon Age Day 21   Moon Sign Libra

A new working week dawns for many Pisceans but it might find you not inclined to become involved in anything complicated. This is a good day for planning but less useful for actually doing much at all. If you can force yourself to take a broad overview of life and organise some activities for later, so much the better.

9 TUESDAY
Moon Age Day 22   Moon Sign Libra

Today could turn out to be a time when you choose to please yourself. Don't get too tied up with domestic issues, most of which will sort themselves out if you give them time. Instead, do something that you really find interesting and enjoyable and be with people whose presence always makes you happy.

10 WEDNESDAY *Moon Age Day 23 Moon Sign Scorpio*

Thinking things through is something you actively choose to do at the moment. You are fairly sociable but may be inclined to withdraw from large groups of people or situations that put you in the spotlight. Look after your money carefully today and only spend when you know you are getting a bargain.

11 THURSDAY *Moon Age Day 24 Moon Sign Scorpio*

A period of significant financial gain could be coming along now. Ideas you had in the past are now likely to mature. Avoid worrying too much about situations you can't control and make certain you feather your own nest as well as those of everyone you know. This is about as selfish as Pisces ever gets so make the most of it.

12 FRIDAY *Moon Age Day 25 Moon Sign Scorpio*

You should feel rather more in tune with life now, thanks in part to the efforts of friends, many of whom seem to be doing all they can to please you right now. The welfare of others is especially close to your heart under today's influences and you could be taking on some challenges soon in the name of charity.

13 SATURDAY *Moon Age Day 26 Moon Sign Sagittarius*

Count on the support of relatives, friends and even some strangers this weekend. Unlike a few days ago, when you were probably quite keen to stick around places you know, now the urge to explore is growing within you. By the evening, you might find that you need to arbitrate between a couple of warring parties.

14 SUNDAY *Moon Age Day 27 Moon Sign Sagittarius*

You should enjoy good conversation today and can also find your romantic world looking very bright. By the evening you will probably be feeling very much like an outing and this could well be with friends. Someone you previously counted as only an acquaintance is likely to be joining your circle before very long.

75

15 MONDAY   *Moon Age Day 28   Moon Sign Capricorn*

The first day of the working week should find you chatty, bright and more than willing to join in. Some of the would-be woes from an earlier time have disappeared like the morning mist, leaving you anxious to have a good time. It is worth keeping your ears open today because even gossip has something to teach you.

16 TUESDAY   *Moon Age Day 0   Moon Sign Capricorn*

Your ability to find friends and to influence people is noteworthy today and you should not avoid any opportunity that comes along to make more of yourself. Your confidence remains essentially high and the slightly retiring qualities of Pisces don't seem to be on display now, quite the contrary in fact.

17 WEDNESDAY   *Moon Age Day 1   Moon Sign Capricorn*

Look for a change of scenery if you really want to keep smiling today. You won't be at all happy with being kept in the same place and diversity is what really fires off your imagination at this time. Mental and intellectual matters are uppermost in your thoughts and you would be incredible at solving puzzles now.

18 THURSDAY   *Moon Age Day 2   Moon Sign Aquarius*

Information coming your way from a friend or associate could do much to brighten your day. Your state of mind generally can be improved as a result of social possibilities that are coming your way now. Romance cannot be ruled out as being an important, and even essential, component in your life right now.

19 FRIDAY   *Moon Age Day 3   Moon Sign Aquarius*

You ought now to be in a better position when it comes to organising your life generally. By tomorrow the Moon will have moved into your own sign and you are going to be very busy indeed. Filling your hours today certainly is not going to be hard but most of your efforts should be of a planning sort.

20 SATURDAY
Moon Age Day 4   Moon Sign Pisces

The Moon enters your zodiac sign, bringing one of the most productive and generally lucky periods of the month. Whatever you take on today, go for gold. Don't be shy of letting people know you are around and show even those people who think they know you well that there is more to you than meets the eye.

21 SUNDAY
Moon Age Day 5   Moon Sign Pisces

There may be little time to rest this Sunday but this should not worry you much at all. You are at your best when out and about and certainly would not take kindly to being cooped up in the same place all day. Trends suggest that a little good luck is in your side and might bring a few surprises by the later part of the day.

22 MONDAY
Moon Age Day 6   Moon Sign Pisces

There are likely to be some serious professional considerations to bear in mind right now and that might mean standing still for a while in order to think. This could go against the grain because you want to get on but it would not be sensible to fail to consider all the options before you decide to proceed in a certain way.

23 TUESDAY
Moon Age Day 7   Moon Sign Aries

Expect plenty of interaction with others. Most of this is going to be interesting and stimulating but you probably won't get on equally well with everyone. Your confidence is high and you believe you are doing the right thing, and that's good because you won't get a chance to think situations through as much as you would generally wish.

24 WEDNESDAY
Moon Age Day 8   Moon Sign Aries

You might have to learn to use a little more concentration when it comes to assessing the needs of those around you. This is a strange statement to make to anyone born under the zodiac sign of Pisces, which is the most caring sign of them all. However, for today the position of the Moon is doing you few favours.

25 THURSDAY   *Moon Age Day 9   Moon Sign Taurus*

New input should be welcomed with open arms around this time. This is a great time for making new contacts, whether these are people you seek for yourself or not. Everyone seems to want to be your friend at the moment and there is no reason to feel quite as nervous about situations as you sometimes do.

26 FRIDAY   *Moon Age Day 10   Moon Sign Taurus*

Now there is much to keep you happy, busy and on the go. You probably will not have the time to think about things too deeply and that could turn out to be a major factor in some of your successes. You are thinking on your feet and that has to be positive when it comes to making personal achievements.

27 SATURDAY   *Moon Age Day 11   Moon Sign Gemini*

There are now exciting social possibilities to look at, though not for long because today really depends on acting quickly. You can have a really good time in the company of people who have a very casual attitude to life. Sometimes this is good for a person who is generally a very deep thinker.

28 SUNDAY   *Moon Age Day 12   Moon Sign Gemini*

Social invitations are likely to come thick and fast now and they bring with them the chance to really enjoy what the weekend, and Sunday in particular, has to offer. If you have been looking for love, it is quite possible you will find it under present trends. Don't give in if there is something you really want.

29 MONDAY   *Moon Age Day 13   Moon Sign Cancer*

Avoid unnecessary assumptions and bear in mind that you could be rather susceptible to deceptions and hidden schemes around now. This would not be a good time to sign any documents unless you are certain of the small print. Confidences from friends need to be strictly kept at this time.

30 TUESDAY *Moon Age Day 14   Moon Sign Cancer*

You really do need to get your act together in a professional sense if you want to take full advantage of some offer that is about to come your way. It is possible that you will doubt yourself, which is a pity because you seem to be on top form and can excel in situations that will puzzle those around you.

31 WEDNESDAY *Moon Age Day 15   Moon Sign Leo*

Don't believe everything you hear from others at the moment and then you won't be too disappointed when things don't go the way you might have wished. You are likely to have a reserve strategy under all circumstances now and this would be wise. It is possible that some Pisceans may have to confront an old demon now.

February

2018

1 THURSDAY
Moon Age Day 16   Moon Sign Leo

Recent small successes could develop into much more, just as long as you concentrate and don't allow others to make either the running or the decisions. You are astute and sharp-thinking at present and you have a strong instinct for what is the right action in any given situation. As a result, your level of confidence grows.

2 FRIDAY
Moon Age Day 17   Moon Sign Virgo

Things could slow down somewhat now for two reasons. Firstly, the lunar low is around and secondly, the sort of progress you have been making is tied to practical and professional matters. Although some impatience is very likely, you need to show the quieter and more reflective face of your zodiac sign.

3 SATURDAY
Moon Age Day 18   Moon Sign Virgo

This is an excellent time to catch up with your partner and to stay mainly in the bosom of your family. Nobody is forcing you down this road, although the temporary respite should prove to have been extremely useful once the new working week begins. At the back of your mind there is likely to be a good deal of planning and scheming taking place.

4 SUNDAY
Moon Age Day 19   Moon Sign Libra

One or two of your major ambitions may be put on hold but only so you can concentrate more fully on others. With plenty of energy and a determination that is many times what Pisces sometimes experiences, you should be willing to put your own considerations first, a fact that is advantageous at this time.

5 MONDAY   *Moon Age Day 20   Moon Sign Libra*

You are especially sensitive to the feelings of those around you as this new week gets underway. Although you want to please everyone, this won't be possible and it will almost certainly be necessary for you to speak your mind at some stage. Where your finances are concerned, hold on tight to money for the moment.

6 TUESDAY   *Moon Age Day 21   Moon Sign Libra*

Trends move on, and your finances could be stronger today as you take action to consolidate a position you chose last week. In addition, decisions you took some weeks or months ago are now beginning to pay dividends. Friends could be especially reliant on you at present and you will need to find the time to show them your special support.

7 WEDNESDAY   *Moon Age Day 22   Moon Sign Scorpio*

The need for new input is strong around the middle of this week and there isn't much doubt that your curiosity is extremely well honed. You avidly devour even scraps of information that come your way in your attempt to build up a better picture of the future. Allied to these trends is your ever-strengthening intuition.

8 THURSDAY   *Moon Age Day 23   Moon Sign Scorpio*

You enjoy and benefit from a generally lighter touch when dealing with social contacts and family members. Maybe you are relaxing your forward momentum a little because there should be more time this Thursday in which to enjoy yourself. Stay away from boring routines and try to find some excitement.

9 FRIDAY   *Moon Age Day 24   Moon Sign Sagittarius*

If there are any frustrations about today, they are likely to come about as a result of the activities of others. Unfortunately, you will have to take these in your stride because there is very little you can do about them. A mixture of loyalty and Piscean sensitivity are most likely to prevent you from firing back.

10 SATURDAY   *Moon Age Day 25   Moon Sign Sagittarius*

This should be a positive period on the domestic scene. It looks as though you are in for some interesting times with regard to family members, with younger people figuring strongly in your life and your future plans. Although you won't consider yourself to be particularly lucky at the moment, there are some gains possible.

11 SUNDAY   *Moon Age Day 26   Moon Sign Sagittarius*

It looks as though you will be in the best of company at the moment. With newer and better invitations leading you down paths you may not have expected, you will need to be on the ball today. Although you can sometimes be slightly shy in settings with which you are not familiar, this isn't likely to be the case right now.

12 MONDAY   *Moon Age Day 27   Moon Sign Capricorn*

Trends today indicate that Pisceans are quite likely to be thinking about personal issues today and maybe seeking to change the ground rules with regard to a relationship. People you haven't seen for quite some time could be coming back into your life soon, bringing with them some surprising news.

13 TUESDAY   *Moon Age Day 28   Moon Sign Capricorn*

Money-making endeavours are well starred and continue to be so between now and the weekend. Although you won't want to take any chances at all, you do have a sort of astrological guardian angel looking over you. When it comes to putting forward your unique point of view, tell it how it is.

14 WEDNESDAY   *Moon Age Day 29   Moon Sign Aquarius*

Any opportunity to make new and influential business contacts should not be passed by. This is especially true if you are self-employed or in a management position. Offers that are made outside of work may well include social gatherings that you find fascinating. Don't allow shyness to hold you back.

15 THURSDAY   *Moon Age Day 0   Moon Sign Aquarius*

When it comes to dealing with others, there could now be a few obstacles to deal with. Not everyone is behaving in quite the way you would expect and you are perhaps a little touchy at present. There could be occasions today when you will need to exercise that famous Piscean patience, though it won't be easy.

16 FRIDAY   *Moon Age Day 1   Moon Sign Aquarius*

You are probably the best team player on the block at the moment and you won't go short of attention, either in a professional or a personal sense. People love to have you around and recognise you to be one of the most cheerful people they come across. Simply enjoy what the positive trends today have to offer.

17 SATURDAY   *Moon Age Day 2   Moon Sign Pisces*

The Moon returns to your zodiac sign, offering a crackerjack of a day, with plenty to set it apart and no lack of attention coming your way. Now is the time to take a slight chance financially because good luck is likely to be with you. Conforming to expectations might be hard but you can get away with it now.

18 SUNDAY   *Moon Age Day 3   Moon Sign Pisces*

Sunday begins on a very positive note indeed. You should be feeling on top form, your intellect is razor sharp and you are very funny. People actively want to have you around and you might even discover some social opportunities you hadn't thought of previously. Don't be surprised if you are being treated as number one.

19 MONDAY   *Moon Age Day 4   Moon Sign Aries*

It is important to be clearer than ever when it comes to discussing matters with others. Don't leave any doubt whatsoever about your point of view and ensure that everyone you come across knows the way you feel. That aside, there ought to be space and time to simply enjoy yourself at this stage of the week.

20 TUESDAY
Moon Age Day 5   Moon Sign Aries

Your happiness with regard to friendships might seem to be somewhat up and down today. This is likely to be due to the changeable nature of those with whom you come into contact but won't be helped if you are jumping about from foot to foot in your own opinions. Stick to your guns, even when others won't agree, if you are sure you are right.

21 WEDNESDAY
Moon Age Day 6   Moon Sign Taurus

The focus now is on communication. Talking to others as much as possible puts you in the picture with regard to practical and professional matters and ensures that you don't lose your way. Friends should prove to be especially helpful at the moment and show a greater than average desire to help you out.

22 THURSDAY
Moon Age Day 7   Moon Sign Taurus

Your most rewarding area of life now concerns domestic and family issues. This may prevent you from pushing as hard in the professional arena as some might wish but it is really only possible to concentrate fully on one thing a time for now. Don't be too quick to believe a small family issue is serious; it may not be as bad as it first appears.

23 FRIDAY
Moon Age Day 8   Moon Sign Taurus

This is no time to be hiding your talents from others. You need to show everyone what you are capable of and the present position of the Moon in your chart is helpful with this regard. If you stand tall and speak your mind, those with whom you come into contact should automatically believe you.

24 SATURDAY
Moon Age Day 9   Moon Sign Gemini

You may be slightly uncomfortable in certain social situations today but there is no real reason for this state of affairs except your own natural shyness. Self-belief is the key to success and you should find that relatives and friends are offering the sort of compliments that make it possible, if not easy, for you to be positive.

25 SUNDAY   *Moon Age Day 10   Moon Sign Gemini*

Keep track of everything that is happening around you and be certain that you turn your intuition up to full when it comes to assessing the actions and reactions of others. This is particularly important if you have to sign any document or take on any long-term financial commitment. Make sure you are getting value for money.

26 MONDAY   *Moon Age Day 11   Moon Sign Cancer*

You have a strong desire to help others and can prove time and again today that you understand what they are going through. This is the quality of empathy and is one of the most important gifts your zodiac sign has been given. Your popularity is justifiably high and people want to help you in return.

27 TUESDAY   *Moon Age Day 12   Moon Sign Cancer*

Others find you to be generous and loving because Pisces is displaying itself to the world in the best possible light just now. More than a degree of good luck is likely to be attending your actions and it looks as though a specific person who is in a good position to lift your life in some way is noticing you.

28 WEDNESDAY   *Moon Age Day 13   Moon Sign Leo*

There might be emotional matters coming to the surface today that you would prefer to be left in the past. You could be right but on the other hand unless you settle them in your mind, they will simply come back to bother you time and again. This might be the day for a good heart-to-heart talk with your partner or a relative.

March 2018

1 THURSDAY
Moon Age Day 14 Moon Sign Leo

There is plenty to keep you interested today, so the only real problem will be whether or not you have the time to fit in everything that takes your fancy. If a particular task or interest has been tiring you of late, leave it alone and focus upon something new. Family members are likely to be calling upon you for assistance at some stage, too.

2 FRIDAY
Moon Age Day 15 Moon Sign Virgo

The lunar low should not prove particularly potent this month, mainly because you are receiving strong planetary support from other directions. It is possible that some of your plans for the forthcoming weekend will have to be modified and today, as well, may contain a few minor setbacks, though nothing you can't handle.

3 SATURDAY
Moon Age Day 16 Moon Sign Virgo

The year is moving on and it is possible that the weather is beginning to improve. Since you will only vegetate if you hang around at home, how taking about a short trip out somewhere? If you can be in the company of people you find stimulating and interesting, then so much the better.

4 SUNDAY
Moon Age Day 17 Moon Sign Libra

Getting on with work and most practical jobs should prove to be easy enough today, though this probably isn't the most progressive or successful day of the week. As it's a Sunday, this may not trouble you much. One of the problems you might notice is a need to constantly compensate for people who are unwilling or unable to do things correctly in your opinion.

5 MONDAY
Moon Age Day 18   Moon Sign Libra

It looks as though pleasure is on the agenda as a new working week commences. Although you are quite capable of working hard at this time, you will also be willing to take time out to simply enjoy yourself. On the way, you should be able to bring a lot of pleasure to those around you, especially family members.

6 TUESDAY
Moon Age Day 19   Moon Sign Scorpio

The responses you get from others in any situation at present are extremely promising, which is why could turn out to be an excellent day for making suggestions. There are several areas of your life that could be better with a little reorganisation. Now you have the chance to look at specifics and to deal with them.

7 WEDNESDAY
Moon Age Day 20   Moon Sign Scorpio

Peace and quiet might not be all that easy to find, particularly at home. You need to feel more secure but the little spats taking place around you make this difficult. Trying to reason with people seems fraught with complications, though if you make sure you have your thinking head on, you can get through or round setbacks.

8 THURSDAY
Moon Age Day 21   Moon Sign Sagittarius

What matters most about today are the generally good trends influencing the way you communicate with others. Telling people precisely what you think is not at all difficult now and since you are also very diplomatic, you can put even the most direct message across in a very positive and inspiring way.

9 FRIDAY
Moon Age Day 22   Moon Sign Sagittarius

What shows most pointedly right now is your natural curiosity. Anything and everything can capture your fertile imagination and nothing is beneath your need to know. The only caution necessary is that you make sure others don't think you are being nosy – even if that is what actually you are.

10 SATURDAY   *Moon Age Day 23   Moon Sign Sagittarius*

The less pressure you put yourself under today, the better things will turn out. Last weekend wasn't exactly the most inspiring you have ever known but you are now in a much more positive frame of mind. All the same, stick to what really interests and inspires you and leave worries on the backburner until Monday.

11 SUNDAY   *Moon Age Day 24   Moon Sign Capricorn*

The ability to charm others is second nature to you now, which makes this a very good time to ask for things you want. Your generally good-natured view of life is obvious to everyone and it would be difficult for them to refuse you any reasonable request. Look for a definite boost to your love life coming along today too.

12 MONDAY   *Moon Age Day 25   Moon Sign Capricorn*

Money matters are probably on your mind and you may be thinking up ways to economise. As you are generally someone who is careful with finances, it is possible that you are panicking without good cause. This might be a good time to talk things through with your partner or someone in the family who can offer you an unbiased point of view.

13 TUESDAY   *Moon Age Day 26   Moon Sign Aquarius*

What you want at the moment is to get life on an even keel. Accept that this might be difficult. Change and unexpected events are part of the present planetary package. If you fall back on your own reserves, you will be able to cope with anything, though relying too much on the advice of others might lead you into further difficulties.

14 WEDNESDAY   *Moon Age Day 27   Moon Sign Aquarius*

The most competitive side of Pisces now begins to show. It doesn't matter whether you are thinking in terms of sport or even professional matters. You want to strike out and go for gold and in doing so will show a great deal more drive and determination than is often the case for your zodiac sign.

15 THURSDAY   *Moon Age Day 28   Moon Sign Aquarius*

Both work and your social life could see some improvements at the moment. There are few difficulties, except those you identify yourself, some of which don't really exist at all. If you experience any difficulty getting to the end of a task that seems to have lasted for ages, get it done little by little, in amongst more enjoyable jobs.

16 FRIDAY   *Moon Age Day 29   Moon Sign Pisces*

You have been hovering on the brink of significant progress for a few days now. The lunar high offers the extra incentive to take life in your own hands and make it produce what you want. If that means being somewhat more selfish than usual, at least you don't completely forget about the needs of others.

17 SATURDAY   *Moon Age Day 0   Moon Sign Pisces*

With a general lucky streak making itself quite obvious now, you are able to forge ahead with plans and can even surpass your own expectations of yourself. The greatest legacy that comes your way now is confidence, a commodity that Pisces lacks on many occasions. If there is something important to be said today, say it.

18 SUNDAY   *Moon Age Day 1   Moon Sign Aries*

This is the sort of day during which most matters will proceed pretty much as you might expect. Don't be too quick to judge others, either by their actions or through what they are saying. Jumping to conclusions could land you in some hot water, an even more likely scenario if you indulge your tendency to gossip.

19 MONDAY   *Moon Age Day 2   Moon Sign Aries*

The sort of fun you are seeking today might be unavailable but that doesn't mean you should fail to look for it. In fact, you may be able to pep things up yourself and it looks as though you have what it takes to make an impression. Pisces is a very understated sign, which is why you are so noticeable when you do turn up the volume.

20 TUESDAY   *Moon Age Day 3   Moon Sign Aries*

Partnerships improve and it doesn't matter if these are of a professional or a personal nature. Almost anyone can be of use to you at the moment and it is clear that your mixture of intuition and practical common sense is what is leading you forward. Be aware that there are likely to be messages coming along from people you don't see very often today.

21 WEDNESDAY   *Moon Age Day 4   Moon Sign Taurus*

A helping hand can be quite important to you at this time and offers you the chance to get ahead in something you didn't really think you were good at. Seek out those who are in the know and if you are deciding on a new hobby, pastime or occupation, make sure everything is in place before you get started. It's vital to do so.

22 THURSDAY   *Moon Age Day 5   Moon Sign Taurus*

Whenever you are working amongst groups around this time you find you can shine like a bright star. It isn't that you leap to the front and show a determination to be the best of the bunch but rather it is your great co-operation and team spirit that matters. At work you could find rules and regulations to be a drag.

23 FRIDAY   ☿   *Moon Age Day 6   Moon Sign Gemini*

Excellent influences surround love and marriage, so it looks like today is a time when you will be turning to the one you love the most. They in turn will show their affection for you, and might even turn this into some help in a practical way. There are gains coming along at the moment that you definitely didn't expect.

24 SATURDAY   ☿   *Moon Age Day 7   Moon Sign Gemini*

On the whole, life will seem fairly stable, partly thanks to the position of the Sun, which is now entering your solar second house. It's true that some things won't be as exciting as they have been but that won't matter just as long as you remain generally happy. A burst of excitement at some stage today might be difficult to explain.

25 SUNDAY ☿ *Moon Age Day 8* *Moon Sign Cancer*

Something very exciting is at happening. Maybe it's a project you started some time ago or it might just be that you are anxious to get ahead generally. Whatever you undertake, you can now do it with aplomb. There are gains to be made at work and maybe a new job in the pipeline if you are between positions.

26 MONDAY ☿ *Moon Age Day 9* *Moon Sign Cancer*

Money-wise you should discover that things are coming together even better than you expected, perhaps with a long-term plan coming to fruition. Of course this depends whether or not you choose to look at such matters today. Certainly there is plenty else that could occupy your mind and you won't be stuck for exciting ways to have a good time.

27 TUESDAY ☿ *Moon Age Day 10* *Moon Sign Leo*

This could turn out to be an emotionally tense time and a period during which you will have to look at things in a logical way. This isn't always easy for Pisces but it is possible that you are likely to jump to unnecessary conclusions otherwise. If you are in doubt about anything, ask someone you consider to be wise.

28 WEDNESDAY ☿ *Moon Age Day 11* *Moon Sign Leo*

Press ahead with major plans and allow others to do what comes naturally to them. You are inclined to work alongside those you care for, either as friends or relatives, but you can't live their lives for them. In any case, there are times when Pisces needs to think and act in isolation. This is such a period.

29 THURSDAY ☿ *Moon Age Day 12* *Moon Sign Virgo*

This looks like the right time to take your foot off the gas pedal and to coast for a while. You need to take stock and if you are aware that this is the case, the lunar low will have very little bearing on your life as a whole. Even apparently casual conversations can be worth a great deal today, so take any opportunity to chill out with friends.

30 FRIDAY ☿ *Moon Age Day 13   Moon Sign Virgo*

Close a few operations down today, if you can, and plan new ones. Your strategy this month has been great and there isn't much doubt about the positive impression you are making on those around you. What a good day this would be to cuddle up and enjoy the company of the one you care for the most.

31 SATURDAY ☿ *Moon Age Day 14   Moon Sign Libra*

You should steam ahead with most ambitions, particularly if you slowed things down yesterday in order to stand back and look. One of the great potential high spots now comes in terms of your romantic life. Whether you have a settled relationship or not, you won't be able to deny that you feel happy and secure.

April

2018

1 SUNDAY   ☿   *Moon Age Day 15*   *Moon Sign Libra*

The Sun is now in your solar second house, which assists most money-making enterprises. Get your thinking cap on without delay because there could be cash available if you simply take the right approach. In other areas, trends indicate that people you haven't seen for a while should be turning up over the next few days.

2 MONDAY   ☿   *Moon Age Day 16*   *Moon Sign Scorpio*

You might find that it is possible to get the best from both worlds now. The domestic area of your life is likely to be very fulfilling but you can also make significant progress at work. If you have the chance to embark on a journey soon, maybe a long one, you have the means at your disposal to broaden your horizons.

3 TUESDAY   ☿   *Moon Age Day 17*   *Moon Sign Scorpio*

Despite the fact that you keenly feel a number of obligations bearing down on you, today is good for all intellectual pursuits. Your mind is crystal clear and you can get through or around a number of potential obstacles. On the way, you are stretching yourself, which has to be a good thing under present trends.

4 WEDNESDAY   ☿   *Moon Age Day 18*   *Moon Sign Scorpio*

Social and co-operative matters are positively highlighted today and much of the joy you experience comes from what you can do on behalf of others. This is fairly typical of the sign of Pisces and is likely to herald a fulfilling period, during which you feel a sense of rightness and balance.

5 THURSDAY   ☿ *Moon Age Day 19*   *Moon Sign Sagittarius*

Your practical skills are well emphasised at this time. It is possible there are jobs around the house that you will want to undertake yourself, even if you have never tackled them before. With increasing belief in your ability and some positive support from your partner or family members, now is the time to get stuck in.

6 FRIDAY   ☿ *Moon Age Day 20*   *Moon Sign Sagittarius*

Minor pressures are possible today, perhaps relating to demands made of you by family members. This could be a little disappointing because you have been putting so much of your attention into the domestic scene of late. All the same, you are generally cheerful now and tend to take matters in your stride.

7 SATURDAY   ☿ *Moon Age Day 21*   *Moon Sign Capricorn*

Though optimism and positive thinking go a long way at present, they are not enough in themselves to ensure success. What you also need is application, which isn't all that easy to come by. The more sociable side to your nature is showing and, probably understandably you want to go out and have fun.

8 SUNDAY   ☿ *Moon Age Day 22*   *Moon Sign Capricorn*

It is time to get down to business and to look very carefully at the practical side of life. You clearly have your thinking head on at the moment and will be easily able to deal with problems that are stumping others. Planetary trends also put a positive slant on love and romance, though it remains to be seen whether you have the time to notice this.

9 MONDAY   ☿ *Moon Age Day 23*   *Moon Sign Capricorn*

Personal and intimate subject matter brings out the best in you today. It is likely that you will be able to enjoy the support of loved ones, together with special friends in whom you put a high degree of trust. Committing yourself to new projects might not be all that easy today but should prove simpler tomorrow.

10 TUESDAY ☿ *Moon Age Day 24* *Moon Sign Aquarius*

Today's activities could provide a great mental boost. There are some very special people around at the moment and it looks as though one or two of them could get very close to opening the door to your own private Piscean world. Be careful what you say because you might come to regret it later.

11 WEDNESDAY ☿ *Moon Age Day 25* *Moon Sign Aquarius*

What matters for today is your versatility. People are turning to you for help and advice of a sort they feel only you can offer. Trends suggest that the middle of this week may be good from a financial point of view, particularly as a result of actions you took some time ago that are only now bearing fruit.

12 THURSDAY ☿ *Moon Age Day 26* *Moon Sign Pisces*

You have all the support you require today with which to push your ideas forward. Any tendency to retreat into your own little world now disappears and you find yourself happy to be in the social flow and taking your place in the world. The lunar high should also mean that you are on the receiving end of a greater degree of luck.

13 FRIDAY ☿ *Moon Age Day 27* *Moon Sign Pisces*

Competition is easily outwitted as you take on new challenges and are able to see all too clearly the nature of the path that lies before you. On the personal front, the number of compliments coming in at the moment bolsters your confidence and makes you able to react in any situation in a positive and even assertive way.

14 SATURDAY ☿ *Moon Age Day 28* *Moon Sign Pisces*

This is a period during which intimate and private matters should be a source of emotional fulfilment, always an important, if not crucial, factor in the life of Pisceans. There could be reasons to celebrate as a result of events within the family and should this come to pass, you will be the first one to put out the flags.

15 SUNDAY   *Moon Age Day 29   Moon Sign Aries*

You can easily achieve any reasonable objectives you set yourself today, though you could also be inclined to retreat into yourself if you feel threatened in any way. By far the best response to any slight difficulties would be to face them squarely but you may not find this course of action too easy for the moment.

16 MONDAY   *Moon Age Day 0   Moon Sign Aries*

Stability ought to be a fact of life and there are gains coming in as a result of past efforts as well as plans that are just starting to mature now. Consideration for the feelings of others are never far from the front of your mind and that certainly seems to be the case at the moment. Positive influences come from the direction of friends.

17 TUESDAY   *Moon Age Day 1   Moon Sign Taurus*

This should be a slightly more settled time in financial terms and there is new scope for improvement to the fine details of your life. Some Pisceans will be thinking about major changes in terms of home surroundings, with a few even considering the possibility of a change of abode in the very near future.

18 WEDNESDAY   *Moon Age Day 2   Moon Sign Taurus*

Though you are likely to spend rather more than you probably should at this stage of the month, you might also find that some cash is coming in from relatively unexpected directions, which compensates somewhat for what is going out. You can't rely on this trend absolutely though, so still be careful about too much outlay.

19 THURSDAY   *Moon Age Day 3   Moon Sign Gemini*

Trends incline you to be very attracted to the finer things in life right now, though there is also a very spiritual element to your personality that really doesn't care at all about possessions. These are conflicting qualities that you have to resolve as best you can. Meanwhile, friends will be urging you to have a splurge of some sort.

20 FRIDAY *Moon Age Day 4   Moon Sign Gemini*

You should be on top form in all practical matters but now suddenly less inclined to get involved in deep heart-to-hearts. This change of tack isn't all that surprising bearing in mind planetary trends as they stand. If there is any work-based decision that presently needs to be made, today could be the best time.

21 SATURDAY *Moon Age Day 5   Moon Sign Cancer*

The Sun enters your solar third house today so you can expect a month ahead that brings plenty of coming and going. You will show yourself as being chattier than usual and extremely friendly. As far as today is concerned, you are likely to spend some time helping a person for whom you have a soft spot.

22 SUNDAY *Moon Age Day 6   Moon Sign Cancer*

You should be in a much better position to call the shots now, particularly if you happen to be a weekend worker. If you are in a position to relax, it is highly likely that you will find some very dynamic way of doing so. Sporting Pisceans are in the very best position of all and can easily get to the finishing line first.

23 MONDAY *Moon Age Day 7   Moon Sign Leo*

Close ties and personal relationships are once again on your mind and prove to be the most important aspects of the day. It is true that as the day advances you will be looking more and more at practical issues and by the evening you could discover reserves of energy you hadn't recognised earlier in the day.

24 TUESDAY *Moon Age Day 8   Moon Sign Leo*

Idealism is a powerful component to your nature at the best of times but is especially well marked now. You will probably manage to get far more done today than you would have expected and won't be in the least fazed by having to do several different things at the same time. You might have to wait for friends to catch up with you.

97

25 WEDNESDAY *Moon Age Day 9   Moon Sign Virgo*

It would be a good idea to play safe in professional matters and to defer to the wisdom of people who know more about certain facts than you do. Take particular care not to draw the attention of others to your perceived limitations because if they take heed of you, you will lose some of the confidence you have in yourself at the moment.

26 THURSDAY *Moon Age Day 10   Moon Sign Virgo*

Getting your own way in a monetary sense could turn out to be rather easier than you had expected. Simply turn on the charm, put forward a good, reasoned case and wait for the result. A degree of frugality may be necessary in the short-term, if only to prove to others you can practically live on fresh air. The lunar low makes this easier than usual.

27 FRIDAY *Moon Age Day 11   Moon Sign Virgo*

There seems to be no better way of getting ahead than by sticking to what you know for the moment. Although you might want to extend the bounds of the possible, under the present lunar low the best progress comes from being what you are to the best of your ability and not through taking actions that go against the grain.

28 SATURDAY *Moon Age Day 12   Moon Sign Libra*

You can look forward to newcomers in your life, especially on a social level. Although you may want to let the whole world know how much you love a certain person, this might not be the best time to be wearing your heart on your sleeve. Temper your emotions or at least hide them from people you don't think you can trust.

29 SUNDAY *Moon Age Day 13   Moon Sign Libra*

Your domestic and emotional life is put on the backburner because this is a time to get out there into the social mainstream. You might find certain tasks you are expected to undertake to be somewhat intimidating but when the time comes, you handle yourself much better than you might have expected and are justifiably proud of yourself.

30 MONDAY   *Moon Age Day 14   Moon Sign Scorpio*

A critical decision is apt to leave you in two minds about certain issues in your life, most likely those to do with work, rather than home or family. How you reach decisions at present is quite interesting and turns out to be pretty much the toss of a coin. However, even then you will, rightly, only take calculated risks at the moment.

May

2018

1 TUESDAY
Moon Age Day 15   Moon Sign Scorpio

In a strong and optimistic mood today, there isn't much at which you will fail when you also have confidence in your own abilities. People notice the new you and are anxious to back a winner. That increases your popularity and might mean a good deal of attention coming your way during the rest of the week.

2 WEDNESDAY
Moon Age Day 16   Moon Sign Sagittarius

The things you hear others saying can be of tremendous use to today so it bodes well to keep your ears open. Taking the ideas that people around you are talking about, you can build new enterprises of your own. Don't expect to get on well with everyone at the moment, that's almost impossible, but important people should be receptive to you.

3 THURSDAY
Moon Age Day 17   Moon Sign Sagittarius

Don't overreach yourself in terms of your ego. Whenever you go overboard and really begin to show tremendous confidence in yourself, something invariably happens to bring you down to earth. Avoid this eventuality by showing a degree of that Pisces humility right from the start of the day.

4 FRIDAY
Moon Age Day 18   Moon Sign Sagittarius

As far as work and finances are concerned, a high-energy period looks likely to be coming along today. You are extremely positive in your approach, a fact that rubs off on those around you. Co-operative ventures are especially well starred now and your ability to work alongside others has rarely been better.

5 SATURDAY   *Moon Age Day 19   Moon Sign Capricorn*

Turning your attention towards home you discover someone doing all they can to make you feel particularly comfortable. Although this tends to take the wind out of your sails somewhat, you should be pleased by the attention you are receiving and on account of the genuine affection coming your way.

6 SUNDAY   *Moon Age Day 20   Moon Sign Capricorn*

Others will find you to be very talkative today and will find it difficult to keep up with your active mind and quick tongue. You do seem to be experiencing many extremes at present but you cope with them well. Certain family members could prove to be a little argumentative but this will not worry you unduly.

7 MONDAY   *Moon Age Day 21   Moon Sign Aquarius*

What a good day this would be for entertaining at home. It is clear that you are now at your vibrant best when in your own environment and will welcome others with open arms. Maybe you will dream up an impromptu party or a gathering of some other sort. Avoid thinking too much about events beyond your own door now.

8 TUESDAY   *Moon Age Day 22   Moon Sign Aquarius*

There are only so many things you can control at once, so if you are tiring with the strain of it all, delegate some of the responsibility. It looks as though there will be people around who are only too willing to lend you a hand. Meanwhile, look for some new and interesting ways to fill your leisure hours.

9 WEDNESDAY   *Moon Age Day 23   Moon Sign Aquarius*

The potential for attracting money is sluggish now and isn't anywhere near as good as you would like it to be. Still, you can tell yourself that the most important things in life have no monetary value. This is the Piscean spiritual ideal, but it might not prevent you from wanting those new shoes!

10 THURSDAY   *Moon Age Day 24   Moon Sign Pisces*

Now you can speed ahead with your dreams and schemes. Bearing in mind the power of the twelfth house Moon over the last two days, it ought to feel as though you are now rocket assisted. Life is likely to look extremely interesting in the immediate days ahead and all sorts of new incentives and opportunities may present themselves.

11 FRIDAY   *Moon Age Day 25   Moon Sign Pisces*

This is a great period in which to work on new plans and schemes in any area of life. There is ready support waiting around every corner, some of it coming from directions you would never have expected. Even if the going gets tough today, you should be able to prove yourself equal to any reasonable challenge.

12 SATURDAY   *Moon Age Day 26   Moon Sign Aries*

You should be looking and feeling at your best today. Socially and romantically, there are many situations that seem tailor-made to suit your needs so seek out friends or spend quality time with your partner. Confrontations of any sort are now kept to a minimum and romance is number-one on the agenda of many Pisceans.

13 SUNDAY   *Moon Age Day 27   Moon Sign Aries*

You can get the very best from family members and people you care for generally, even though it isn't possible for you to be at home quite as much as you might wish. A lot of the pressure you feel at the moment is related to being in the limelight, a place where you invariably feel ill at ease.

14 MONDAY   *Moon Age Day 28   Moon Sign Taurus*

Quick thinking comes in handy today and you won't have any difficulty functioning at full strength. Your mind works like lightning, though it is also sometimes drawn to places you care for deeply and which you might not have seen for a while. You should be feeling generally comfortable with personal and romantic attachments.

15 TUESDAY
Moon Age Day 0   Moon Sign Taurus

Your mood and general peace of mind is assisted as a result of the actions of loved ones. This is a recurring theme at present and under present planetary trends there is no wonder. You may not feel quite the recent need to be doing something all the time and can quite easily relax in the company of someone you love today.

16 WEDNESDAY
Moon Age Day 1   Moon Sign Gemini

Today you show yourself to be outgoing and enthusiastic, though you could suffer a little from inadequate planning and will need to be careful if someone you consider a rival is not going to get ahead of you. Pisceans who are presently in full time education can expect to be doing well with studies now.

17 THURSDAY
Moon Age Day 2   Moon Sign Gemini

The focus is now upon communications in the world beyond your own front door. A favourable period for important negotiations and discussions, this is a time during which you can get what you want, though only with determination and belief. You may turn your attention to comfort and security later in the day.

18 FRIDAY
Moon Age Day 3   Moon Sign Cancer

Domestic matters could tie you down somewhat right now and you would be best not getting too involved in situations you presently can't or won't alter. Younger people especially could turn out to be quite frustrating in their objectives and desires, some of which directly contradict your own. Piscean patience is called for.

19 SATURDAY
Moon Age Day 4   Moon Sign Cancer

You can afford to be slightly more ambitious in your personal aims and should be going for gold at every possible opportunity. Not everyone is presently on your side it's true but you do have a really good ability to persuade others to follow your lead. It is definitely worth talking, talking and talking again in order to get what you want.

20 SUNDAY
Moon Age Day 5   Moon Sign Leo

Some of the responsibilities coming into you from the outside world won't be all that welcome and you could decide to retreat into yourself a little at the moment. However, sooner or later there are issues that you are going to have to face and it might as well be now as at any time later. Grasp the nettle and have some difficult conversations if they are needed.

21 MONDAY
Moon Age Day 6   Moon Sign Leo

You won't have a great deal of patience with financial restrictions and will really want to feel free and unfettered right now Woe-betide anyone who tries to force you into any sort of mould because it just won't work. Have some patience with family members who are going slightly astray and listen to them.

22 TUESDAY
Moon Age Day 7   Moon Sign Leo

Trends suggest that a communication received may put you in the picture today so it is very important to keep talking, to anyone who will listen and respond. You may be researching something or perhaps involved in higher education. If so, make certain that you concentrate your efforts at the moment because a significant breakthrough is possible.

23 WEDNESDAY
Moon Age Day 8   Moon Sign Virgo

Important decisions are best left alone for the moment, whilst you get on with negotiating the lunar low. Although you shouldn't really notice the Moon in Virgo quite as much this month as at some times, it can bring you to a more thoughtful stage in your life, a fact that your pals and loved ones are apt to notice.

24 THURSDAY
Moon Age Day 9   Moon Sign Virgo

Unexpected delays are possible, allied to awkward people who seem to feel it is their duty to cause you certain headaches. You can deal with all of this and still come out smiling. The fact is that you have the bit between your teeth and it will take more than an adverse position of the Moon to hold you back.

25 FRIDAY   *Moon Age Day 10   Moon Sign Libra*

This would be an excellent time in which to put your persuasive tongue to work. There are people around who are very influenced by what you have to say and this means that at work especially you might be able to move matters forward quite progressively. Even casual conversations can have far-reaching implications.

26 SATURDAY   *Moon Age Day 11   Moon Sign Libra*

Personal and domestic concerns now bring out the best in you, though there are social bonuses around too, probably later in the day. Concern for family members, which could have been running quite high of late is not so marked at present, leaving you extra time to spend this weekend in doing what suits you personally.

27 SUNDAY   *Moon Age Day 12   Moon Sign Scorpio*

Today's trends now indicate that your personal life can be somewhat troubled, although by tomorrow everything is going to look very different, so it is important not to overreact. You may retire into yourself at some stage today but you are merely reacting to temporary trends. Don't be too quick to take offence, especially with a friend.

28 MONDAY   *Moon Age Day 13   Moon Sign Scorpio*

A communication from far away might lift your spirits at the beginning of this week and you will also be chattier than may have been the case for a number of days. There are potential gains to be made from simply being in the right place at the right time but your personal analysis of the situation are also part of the scenario.

29 TUESDAY   *Moon Age Day 14   Moon Sign Sagittarius*

There's more coming along than you bargained for, and most likely in a very positive way. Don't leave anything to chance today and make sure that everyone knows you are around. This is a key day in more than one respect. Not only do you shine when in company but you should also discover talents you didn't know you possessed.

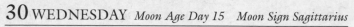

30 WEDNESDAY *Moon Age Day 15   Moon Sign Sagittarius*

The emphasis now is on busy communication, though others might find you just a little too talkative at the moment. It's important not to labour points too much and if you remember the general rule for now, which is to spread yourself around as much as you can, you won't go far wrong. A friend may need some very specific advice.

31 THURSDAY *Moon Age Day 16   Moon Sign Sagittarius*

You will enjoy being with loved ones today and the position of the Sun makes this a likely eventuality for the next two or three weeks. You may not even notice the difference because Pisces tends to be something of a home-bird in any case. Most of what you do today is likely to involve either your partner or family members.

June

2018

1 FRIDAY
Moon Age Day 17   Moon Sign Capricorn

With a slight lull in the pace of activities, your mind could turn once again to house and home. What a good time this would be for entertaining and maybe for throwing a dinner party. Much of the enjoyment you experience today is likely to be associated with domestic rather than professional matters so forget about work once Friday night is underway.

2 SATURDAY
Moon Age Day 18   Moon Sign Capricorn

You are quite likely to prove a more boisterous personality than might have seemed to be the case of late. You stand out in a crowd and can give a very good impression of yourself. It is obvious that you are also quite adventurous at present, not a word that is often seen associated with Pisces. Enjoy the unusual trend and the reaction it provokes.

3 SUNDAY
Moon Age Day 19   Moon Sign Aquarius

Never a dull moment could be your motto this Sunday. Responding more positively today to the position of little Mercury in your solar chart, you are witty, bright and good to know. You may be taking trips down memory lane but these are now somehow more healthy and positive. A little nostalgia is not a bad thing, especially on a quiet Sunday.

4 MONDAY
Moon Age Day 20   Moon Sign Aquarius

There are strong emotional rewards for the taking today, mainly as a result of the position of the Sun in your solar fourth house. If you have not been able to turn your mind towards love and relationships of late, now you should find you have a few hours to spare. Spend time saying much needed words to your partner, or perhaps go out for an enjoyable evening.

5 TUESDAY   *Moon Age Day 21   Moon Sign Aquarius*

Your powers to get things done seem a little ineffectual today, so you may as well decide right at the start to take a little break. This is a time for thinking, with the acting part coming in just a couple of days. Don't be too worried if one or two of your plans seem to be going slightly wrong for now as this is purely a temporary phase.

6 WEDNESDAY   *Moon Age Day 22   Moon Sign Pisces*

With strong supporting planetary trends and the Moon paying your zodiac sign a visit, now is the moment to act. Objectives that have been in your mind for some time move forward at a pace, whilst at the same time you show yourself and everyone around you how dynamic and decisive you can be. Go for gold, Pisces!

7 THURSDAY   *Moon Age Day 23   Moon Sign Pisces*

The green light is still on and you find this a good time to make tracks, as well as gaining invaluable assistance on the way. General good luck attends your actions and offers you the chance to achieve something that has been at the back of your mind for a while. Even if life isn't easy, it should be very interesting.

8 FRIDAY   *Moon Age Day 24   Moon Sign Aries*

Look out for some overall improvements at work, or perhaps a better ability to concentrate if you are presently in education. The better times are really down to you and the way your mind is presently working. Don't be too quick to listen to gossip today because much of it isn't really worth the effort and it could lead to some misunderstandings.

9 SATURDAY   *Moon Age Day 25   Moon Sign Aries*

It looks as though there will be few dull moments this weekend, as the general pace of activity increases. You have a great deal of skill when it comes to getting others to follow your lead and you won't be short of fine words in any situation. Change and diversity is what counts at the moment.

10 SUNDAY *Moon Age Day 26 Moon Sign Aries*

Personal relationships could be somewhat less harmonious than you would wish, although this fact doesn't seem to have a great deal to do with you. It's important to speak the truth at the moment, even if that means upsetting someone else. All the same, you can find ways to be tactful so choose your words carefully.

11 MONDAY *Moon Age Day 27 Moon Sign Taurus*

Since professional matters appear to be progressive enough, the chances are you will want to put some pep into your out-of-work activities. Concern for the underdog is big in your thinking right now, as it often is, and you can expect to have your usual Piscean concern for charities that support people who are having a hard time in their life.

12 TUESDAY *Moon Age Day 28 Moon Sign Taurus*

The position of some planets in your chart today indicates that some of your plans are now reaching a critical phase and you won't want to relinquish control to anyone else. This influence can directly interact with another – the need to share. Out of these conflicting interests you manage to forge a way forward that pleases you and everyone.

13 WEDNESDAY *Moon Age Day 0 Moon Sign Gemini*

A new phase of high spirits and joviality comes along. Pisces has many positive aspects surrounding it right now and you are in a great position to make the most of this. As much as anything, it is the way your mind is working that offers new incentives and ways to pass on the happiness you feel to those around you.

14 THURSDAY *Moon Age Day 1 Moon Sign Gemini*

Much of your energy today is piled into situations you see as being personally important. It is just possible that this means less attention being put in the direction of family members. It would be good to offer a little reassurance because those you love are very used to seeing your warm and attentive side.

109

15 FRIDAY   *Moon Age Day 2   Moon Sign Cancer*

The focus now is definitely on your love life and romance generally. This is likely to be a very definite 'up' period with much of what you have been looking for likely to come your way. Don't spoil this by spending more time than you must out there in a more practical and go-getting world.

16 SATURDAY   *Moon Age Day 3   Moon Sign Cancer*

Relations with family members are now strengthened by a number of astrological factors and if there is something you need to ask for in the way of a favour, this could be the best time of all in which to do it. Relying on friends can be less advisable for today at least because they may be too busy to lend assistance.

17 SUNDAY   *Moon Age Day 4   Moon Sign Leo*

You could now be pulled between your desire to be with loved ones and your need to make contact with the outside world. There isn't much that makes you feel really wonderful for now but this is a state of affairs that won't last long. Personalities of one sort or another might be entering your life sometime soon.

18 MONDAY   *Moon Age Day 5   Moon Sign Leo*

You should prove to be more than modestly successful in almost anything you choose to take on at the moment. Your chart for the next few days does not indicate that you will be getting ahead professionally, so why not ring the changes altogether and get away from everything? What a good time this would be to take a break.

19 TUESDAY   *Moon Age Day 6   Moon Sign Virgo*

Keep your life today as free from complications as you can manage. There are some demands coming your way but as long as you are not expecting too much of yourself, you should be able to manage. Some Pisceans are withdrawing into their shells at present so don't expect to be wonderful company.

20 WEDNESDAY   *Moon Age Day 7   Moon Sign Virgo*

It could feel as if you are taking one step forward in life today but two steps back. By tomorrow, the Moon will have moved on and any little cloud that seems to be hovering over your head will have lifted so there is no real need to be out of sorts. Keep it simple and quiet and you won't even notice the lunar low.

21 THURSDAY   *Moon Age Day 8   Moon Sign Libra*

A period of intense feelings and emotional conflicts may take you by surprise, though this will have less of a part to play in your life if you are aware that it is coming along. Don't rise to the bait of someone who is spoiling for a row and then you will be the winner from the word go. At work you may need to do the same job more than once.

22 FRIDAY   *Moon Age Day 9   Moon Sign Libra*

The domestic scene tends to be not only fairly hectic but also quite rewarding as the working week draws to a close for many Pisceans. You may not get exactly what you want in a professional sense but you can be sure that those you care about the most are showing a great deal of affection and offering much help.

23 SATURDAY   *Moon Age Day 10   Moon Sign Scorpio*

You are friendly and affectionate to just about everyone but particularly to someone who has proved to be especially loyal of late. Anything historic or ancient could have a specific fascination for you at the moment and your intuitive or even psychic side is really showing. Unusual forms of entertainment attract you now.

24 SUNDAY   *Moon Age Day 11   Moon Sign Scorpio*

A most agreeable period is about to start. You need to take advantage of it by being in the company of your romantic partner or good friends. Social trends look particularly good and there's no doubt at all about your personal charm at this time. Stay away from controversy of any sort for the next couple of days, though.

25 MONDAY   *Moon Age Day 12   Moon Sign Scorpio*

Along comes a boost to for your personal life in which leisure pursuits are highlighted and it looks as though you can get the most from any sort of social gathering. Although you still may not be quite as adventurous as you might like to be, you can gain from meeting new people and thinking about becoming involved in different interests.

26 TUESDAY   *Moon Age Day 13   Moon Sign Sagittarius*

Your confidence is increasing and the Sun, now in your solar fifth house, is part of the reason for this. You tend to get your own way quite easily in romantic matters and from the point of view of general leisure and pleasure could well be starting out on a new phase. Socially speaking you are good to know.

27 WEDNESDAY   *Moon Age Day 14   Moon Sign Sagittarius*

You may have exciting and unusual social and romantic possibilities before you. Your persuasive powers are very good at the moment and you can be of special use to a family member who has been having problems of late. The way you look at life and your sense of fun are very infectious at present.

28 THURSDAY   *Moon Age Day 15   Moon Sign Capricorn*

This would be a very good time for co-operative and collaborative endeavours of almost any sort. Even though you feel you are doing very well it is possible that someone will not believe you are pulling your weight and some extra effort might seem to be necessary to convince them. Actually, you have nothing to prove.

29 FRIDAY   *Moon Age Day 16   Moon Sign Capricorn*

Getting your own way at the moment is generally a matter of turning on the charm, which is never difficult for Pisces. You are displaying the very best of what you can be and so should enjoy a really good day. Events may prove to be spiritually enlightening, though pleasures are probably very simple.

30 SATURDAY   *Moon Age Day 17   Moon Sign Capricorn*

You need to find time today to go off and explore the world as much as you can. There is plenty to see and any number of interesting people around to see it with. This is not a Saturday during which practical or professional matters should be allowed to get in the way of simply doing what seems like special fun.

July

2018

1 SUNDAY
Moon Age Day 18   Moon Sign Aquarius

You definitely benefit from taking a hands-on approach in almost any situation right now. Although you may be feeling a little cautious and certainly not inclined to rush into anything, all in all you can make great progress. Romance isn't out of the question, even if you haven't necessarily been expecting it.

2 MONDAY
Moon Age Day 19   Moon Sign Aquarius

You should now be in a light and optimistic mood, anxious to get to know new people but also very attentive to family members and friends. With such a sociable period in operation, it might be rather difficult to actually get anything done in a concrete sense. Never mind, you can split your time and make space for everyone who needs you.

3 TUESDAY
Moon Age Day 20   Moon Sign Pisces

It is unlikely you will have to work very hard to win anyone's support today. The Moon is in your zodiac sign and there are several other planetary positions working in your favour. If you can't get through everything you want to do quickly enough to leave time for fun, leave some of it until later. Pleasing yourself is your ultimate goal, especially this evening.

4 WEDNESDAY
Moon Age Day 21   Moon Sign Pisces

Along come renewed vitality, a determination to succeed and far more drive than has sometimes been the case so far this year. This is potentially a day for good luck, even if you are actually creating some of it for yourself. There are gains to be made at work, perhaps as a result of the influence you have on others.

5 THURSDAY   *Moon Age Day 22   Moon Sign Pisces*

Certain personal or practical arrangements could quite easily be subject to delay now. Don't let this bother you but remain flexible in your attitude and willing to take a different path at very short notice and all will be well. Casual conversations can bring unexpected news or some really good ideas you will soon be bursting to put into practice.

6 FRIDAY   *Moon Age Day 23   Moon Sign Aries*

Stick around familiar faces today because you are not quite as adventurous as turned out to be the case a couple of days ago. Although you are by no means a shrinking violet, you could be rather inclined to hide behind the bigger personalities of friends. But it doesn't matter what you do, there are people who want to know you better.

7 SATURDAY   *Moon Age Day 24   Moon Sign Aries*

Impressing others isn't too difficult today and you manage to pull the right rabbit out of the hat when it is important to do so. People will trust you a great deal and you might worry just a little in case you let them down. This is most unlikely to happen. Just be yourself and do what feels right.

8 SUNDAY   *Moon Age Day 25   Moon Sign Taurus*

When it matters the most you can rely on your instincts today, which are most unlikely to let you down. A few financial pressures are possible this Sunday but there are many things you can do that are absolutely free, or which cost very little. Being with friends would be good but even better times involve your partner.

9 MONDAY   *Moon Age Day 26   Moon Sign Taurus*

The accent is now less on practical organisation and more on initiative and willpower. Very little will hold you back at present, at least not once you have made up your mind. You may have to use slightly unorthodox ways of getting what you want from the day but the chances are that you will win through.

10 TUESDAY   *Moon Age Day 27   Moon Sign Gemini*

Progress is likely to be swift now, mainly because you work hard to get things done. It doesn't matter whether there is a professional aspect to today or not, simply because your capacity for work demonstrates itself as much at home as it does anywhere else. Don't forget that you also need to have some fun.

11 WEDNESDAY   *Moon Age Day 28   Moon Sign Gemini*

Get out and travel as much as you can today. You won't take kindly to being stuck indoors and you can gain tremendously from seeing new places, as well as from meeting people you haven't come across before. If at all possible, avoid taking on an excessively stressful workload and delegate if it is possible to do so.

12 THURSDAY   *Moon Age Day 29   Moon Sign Cancer*

There are positive social highlights and generally uplifting trends to be experienced at this stage of the week. Your powers of communication are good and it is clear you are in the mood for debate. Co-operative ventures of any sort are especially well accented at this time, so look for a social partner or group to join if you can.

13 FRIDAY   *Moon Age Day 0   Moon Sign Cancer*

At work, your progress can be little short of fantastic, though you have to give much of what you are to the task at hand and could become slightly fatigued by the end of the day. When social hours beckon, spend some time in the company of people whose presence always has the power to relax you.

14 SATURDAY   *Moon Age Day 1   Moon Sign Leo*

Your ability to show a distinctly practical face to the world at large is inclined to fall flat today. You will need to rely on the help, support and advice that comes from the direction of people you know and trust. During this minor interlude, you should concentrate on having fun if you possibly can.

15 SUNDAY   *Moon Age Day 2   Moon Sign Leo*

Having friends close to you now is very important and makes you feel better about yourself. Although there could be one or two slightly sticky situations to get through today, you keep a smile on your face and show how positive you are capable of being. In truth, your confidence might be lacking but nobody would ever guess.

16 MONDAY   *Moon Age Day 3   Moon Sign Virgo*

You can't really expect to be at your most communicative today. The lunar low takes away some of your determination and might make it somewhat difficult to achieve the direct contact with others you might wish. More withdrawn, your attitude is one of patience and your technique is to organise behind the scenes. This is not a bad plan at all today.

17 TUESDAY   *Moon Age Day 4   Moon Sign Virgo*

Don't be surprised if there are some setbacks today, particularly with regard to projects you see as being important to your future. The delays will almost certainly be very temporary but they have to be recognised. Instead of trying to plough on with things you can't do, concentrate on something that you are able to complete.

18 WEDNESDAY   *Moon Age Day 5   Moon Sign Libra*

Though the nostalgic side of your nature is stimulated at this time, you will also want to get on with something practical. The two states of mind don't really go hand in hand and this could mean some slight confusion. By the evening you should have resolved the conundrums and will settle for peace and quiet.

19 THURSDAY   *Moon Age Day 6   Moon Sign Libra*

This is a time during which it is not sensible to force issues too much, especially in the material world. You need to work hard in order to get what you want but you still have to go with the flow. Any tendency to push too hard is likely to be self-defeating and actually achieve the opposite of what you intended.

20 FRIDAY   *Moon Age Day 7   Moon Sign Libra*

You should be feeling both enthusiastic and competitive, which is why today offers so much. Life is quite often down to a state of mind. If you believe you are equal to a particular task – you most probably are. Today you can break the bounds of the possible and even surprise yourself on the way. Hold nothing back today, Pisces!

21 SATURDAY   *Moon Age Day 8   Moon Sign Scorpio*

It seems that industry and general hard work is the order of the day but not because anyone is forcing you down this path. There are astrological trends about that increase your level of energy and which make you ever more determined to win through to objectives that might have seemed impossible only months ago.

22 SUNDAY   *Moon Age Day 9   Moon Sign Scorpio*

On the day the Sun enters your solar sixth house, you can expect to experience a boost to your health and feelings of general wellbeing. If you have been off colour, this position of the Sun is quite likely to help. Practical projects and plans for the future are also aided by the presence of the Sun here.

23 MONDAY   *Moon Age Day 10   Moon Sign Sagittarius*

Focus on relationships today, and especially those that are most important to you. There won't be much difficulty in coming to terms with practical issues but from an emotional point of view you may be rather too sensitive for your own good. If you can, settle for some way of enjoying yourself that is not too physically demanding.

24 TUESDAY   *Moon Age Day 11   Moon Sign Sagittarius*

This is a time when you may find yourself getting tied up with material considerations, some of which might go against the grain somewhat. Nevertheless you need to think about money and the way you are going to get more of it in the months ahead. Make sure you set some time aside for enjoyment too, if you want to avoid a headache.

25 WEDNESDAY   *Moon Age Day 12   Moon Sign Capricorn*

A new social contact or an existing friend might do you a great favour now and you will need to think up a unique way of saying thank you. Meet as many different people as you can at the moment and make the most of extremely good trends that involve doing little more than enjoying yourself alongside others.

26 THURSDAY   *Moon Age Day 13   Moon Sign Capricorn*

Don't let others get hold of the wrong end of the stick at this time. Explaining yourself and your ideas as fully as you can is now extremely important. Someone you don't see very often is likely to be making an appearance around now and there might be the opportunity to make a trip that is planned at very short notice.

27 FRIDAY   *Moon Age Day 14   Moon Sign Capricorn*

You start to see really good opportunities for gain, both in a material and a personal sense. This is the time of the month during which you are filled with excellent ideas. Conforming to expectations might go against the grain but you won't go short of the right sort of company when it comes to diversions of any sort.

28 SATURDAY   *Moon Age Day 15   Moon Sign Aquarius*

Stay close to familiar faces and places this weekend. You will be happiest when in the company of people who make you feel comfortable. You will be feeling particularly sensitive to the needs of those around you and will be displaying all the empathy your sign is capable of mustering. Your creative potential is also now particularly good.

29 SUNDAY   *Moon Age Day 16   Moon Sign Aquarius*

Your love life has its bonuses now but you don't need to try too hard to bring others round to your way of thinking. Don't expect anything too outrageous today. In the main you are happy to accept what comes along and as you are not going to be a great pace-setter at the end of this month, that's just as well.

30 MONDAY   *Moon Age Day 17   Moon Sign Pisces*

As the Moon moves into your zodiac sign you find yourself in a
positive frame of mind and anxious to get on with things. You now
have an abundance of confidence and you won't have any problems
bringing people round to your point of view. Best of all, you
recognise how important you are to those you hold dear.

31 TUESDAY   *Moon Age Day 18   Moon Sign Pisces*

Not only the people you know but also individuals you have barely
met before conspire to give you a good day. This is not a time for
routines and the lunar high demands that you put in that extra bit of
effort that can make all the difference. With good luck on your side,
getting along well is easy right now.

August 2018

1 WEDNESDAY ☿ *Moon Age Day 19   Moon Sign Pisces*

You can't afford to take anything for granted on a practical level and therefore need to check all details carefully. If it appears that someone is deliberately throwing obstacles in your path, be sure of your facts before you say or do something you may regret. You could discover you are being somewhat paranoid at present.

2 THURSDAY ☿ *Moon Age Day 20   Moon Sign Aries*

The workplace is favoured by trends in your chart at the moment and there might not be quite as much time to spend with your partner or loved ones as you would wish. Specific trends can now make you somewhat absent-minded, so it's important to make a note of birthdays or anniversaries that might be in the offing between now and the weekend.

3 FRIDAY ☿ *Moon Age Day 21   Moon Sign Aries*

You can find very interesting things to do with yourself at this time and won't easily be convinced that any of your ideas are unworkable. The problem could be that one or two of them actually are, and those who care for you the most realise this. Employ a listening ear and try to look at your life objectively.

4 SATURDAY ☿ *Moon Age Day 22   Moon Sign Taurus*

Home is the best and most comfortable place for Pisces to be at present, so this weekend probably won't see you moving around very much. You are quite creative at the moment so will probably be working in your house or garden. A degree of personal contentment is present at this time.

5 SUNDAY ☿ *Moon Age Day 23 Moon Sign Taurus*

This is still a good period to be making the sort of progress you are definitely looking for right now. You show good and promising judgement in all matters and won't easily be put off once you have made up your mind to follow a particular path. Inspiration is part of the present package for Pisces.

6 MONDAY ☿ *Moon Age Day 24 Moon Sign Gemini*

Don't allow yourself to become involved in needless debates, which won't help your cause and can only serve to confuse already problematic situations. There is almost certainly help on offer if you want it, though you are likely to be relying on your own efforts and judgement now and so may decide to continue going it alone.

7 TUESDAY ☿ *Moon Age Day 25 Moon Sign Gemini*

The smooth running of practical affairs today is your chief concern, as indeed seems to have been the case for a while now. Although circumstances force you to work within certain confines, you are presently extremely good at solving problems and won't easily be distracted, even by people you do not always have the greatest respect for.

8 WEDNESDAY ☿ *Moon Age Day 26 Moon Sign Gemini*

Help seems available to you today, no matter what you decide to do. There are times when you are responding to necessity rather than to choice but you can make these times enjoyable too. Routines could be a bore, which is why you are likely to be doing your best to ring the changes as much as you can.

9 THURSDAY ☿ *Moon Age Day 27 Moon Sign Cancer*

In personal relationships, it is important not to get too wrapped up in your own ideas, no matter how entrancing they seem to you. Use a listening ear and be willing to modify your plans to compromise with your partner if necessary. A final word of warning for a summer Thursday: avoid staying in the same place for too long at a time.

122

10 FRIDAY ☿ *Moon Age Day 28 Moon Sign Cancer*

This is looking likely to be the best period for financial gain during August. You tend to act very much on impulse but your sense of humour is fully in place and so if you make a mistake, you can laugh your way out of it. Caring as always, your concern for the underdog is particularly strong at the moment.

11 SATURDAY ☿ *Moon Age Day 0 Moon Sign Leo*

You are likely to be speaking your mind today, which is fine, as long as you know what you are talking about. Don't get tied down by too many details but try to look at the broader picture of life. Where a whole series of tasks are concerned, do them one at a time and take note of your progress.

12 SUNDAY ☿ *Moon Age Day 1 Moon Sign Leo*

It could be that practical duties are something of a bind today, which is why you tend to shrug them off or delegate someone else to do them if you have the chance. However, there is no way of avoiding certain responsibilities, so you will just have to grit your teeth and get them done as quickly as possible.

13 MONDAY ☿ *Moon Age Day 2 Moon Sign Virgo*

This is a day when you will notice certain limitations, especially within relationships. As always, you are inclined to look at things less sensibly during the period of the lunar low, so the advice is to take what comes and to avoid reacting as if things are never going to work out well for you again. You know in your heart that this is not the case.

14 TUESDAY ☿ *Moon Age Day 3 Moon Sign Virgo*

Important decisions are best left until later. Your expectations of what life holds for you might as well be kept to a minimum, because your imaginative processes are not too well-honed right now. Settle for a slow and steady sort of day and accept what comes along. If you do, there's a quiet sort of enjoyment to be had.

15 WEDNESDAY ☿   *Moon Age Day 4   Moon Sign Libra*

Now is as good a time as any to take your life into your own hands. You clearly know what you want and have a very good idea about how you are going to get it. Even apparently unfortunate events can be turned to your advantage and will give you a bit of a head start at this stage of August.

16 THURSDAY ☿   *Moon Age Day 5   Moon Sign Libra*

This is the start of what should turn out to be one of the most dynamic periods of the month. You certainly work best now as part of a co-operative team and will be adding a great many good ideas to the pile. Some Pisceans will be choosing this time to look very carefully into their roots and family background.

17 FRIDAY ☿   *Moon Age Day 6   Moon Sign Scorpio*

The Sun, still in your solar sixth house, helps to boost practical issues and might make you slightly better off than you had thought. You invest all your efforts now with extra zing and will be good to know. The genteel side of Pisces might be taking something of a holiday but you could hardly be considered crude at this time.

18 SATURDAY ☿   *Moon Age Day 7   Moon Sign Scorpio*

There could be some tensions in what are normal discussions, partly because you are not looking as fairly at other people's points of view as might usually be the case. Try to stay away from too much decision-making and do what you can to promote a fairly easy-going sort of weekend. Friends expect your help and you will be there for them.

19 SUNDAY   *Moon Age Day 8   Moon Sign Sagittarius*

Your ego is bigger than it would usually be today and it is possible that others will get the wrong end of the stick as far as you are concerned. Try to show your easy-going face to the world and don't allow situations to annoy you. When it comes to family arguments, remember that it takes two to tango and you don't have to be in the dance.

20 MONDAY   *Moon Age Day 9   Moon Sign Sagittarius*

This is a time when it is much easier to develop a stronger will, particularly with regard to issues you see as being important to you in a professional sense. If you have been looking for a new career move, today might be a good time to keep your eyes and ears open. People should prove to be very friendly.

21 TUESDAY   *Moon Age Day 10   Moon Sign Sagittarius*

You don't mind hard work at the moment and will be quite willing to do whatever is necessary to get what you want from life in a general sense. Today may offer you the chance to mix with people you haven't come across before and might also bring you closer to realising an ambition. Open your mind to all sorts of opportunities now.

22 WEDNESDAY   *Moon Age Day 11   Moon Sign Capricorn*

You are a sharp thinker right now but you could have a tendency to get rather impatient with people whose thought processes don't match your own. This is quite unusual because you are generally the most patient person imaginable. Don't be too quick to jump to conclusions, especially in professional matters.

23 THURSDAY   *Moon Age Day 12   Moon Sign Capricorn*

Your efforts to get ahead in a general sense now look like bearing fruit. Your level of energy is stepped up and there are people around you all the time now who have similar ideas to your own. There is no reason at all why you shouldn't feel on top form, both at work and in a social sense, and be achieving all you want to.

24 FRIDAY   *Moon Age Day 13   Moon Sign Aquarius*

You are now absorbing news and views at a fantastic rate and will want to be certain that everyone knows your opinions. Good to know and great to have around, it looks as though present astrological trends are offering you one of the most potent periods you will experience during August.

25 SATURDAY   *Moon Age Day 14   Moon Sign Aquarius*

This is a good period for useful information gathering and you won't have any difficulty being considered for advancement of some sort, be it at work or socially. Although yours is sometimes a fairly retiring sort of zodiac sign, this does not turn out to be the case right now and your personality is sparkling.

26 SUNDAY   *Moon Age Day 15   Moon Sign Aquarius*

You now develop very strong feelings about certain aspects of the past and will also definitely feel the need to be around people who make you feel confident. Through the whole of the recent spell of dynamic thoughts and actions, the slightly hesitant side of Pisces has been around as well and it shows even more today.

27 MONDAY   *Moon Age Day 16   Moon Sign Pisces*

Personal and professional objectives alike now appear in stark and obvious clarity. You know what you want and how to get it. It is easy to do yourself, or anyone else, a favour whilst you are in this frame of mind. A very modest flutter might be in order, since the lunar high is around, but make it so modest that you don't mind if you lose.

28 TUESDAY   *Moon Age Day 17   Moon Sign Pisces*

Most initiatives work out the way you would wish but it might be nice to concentrate on having a great time, rather than trying to push any particular issue. You are the life and soul of any party, especially as you are likely to be the one throwing it! Consideration for others is paramount in all your thoughts and actions today.

29 WEDNESDAY   *Moon Age Day 18   Moon Sign Aries*

A few of your ideas might prove to be somewhat over-ambitious and might have to fall by the wayside as a result. In the main you pick up one or two schemes and run with them very successfully indeed. The attitude of people you don't know very well can puzzle you unless you ask a few questions.

30 THURSDAY   *Moon Age Day 19   Moon Sign Aries*

You will discover that one-to-one relationships are the attachments you will want to explore fully around this time. You might be taking something of a holiday from the real pressures coming at you from professional demands and would be willing today to allow others to take a good deal of the strain.

31 FRIDAY   *Moon Age Day 20   Moon Sign Aries*

Co-operative discussions are the most productive ones for now and although there is some incentive to go it alone, this is not the right way forward. Once you get into the swing of things you should enjoy all that today has to offer and you certainly won't be inclined to stay in the shadows, as is sometimes the case.

September 2018

1 SATURDAY   *Moon Age Day 21   Moon Sign Taurus*

There could be a slightly hot-tempered aspect to relationships today, at least part of which is because of your attitude. Unfortunately, you presently have the planet Mars in a potentially volatile position and this means that on occasions you will have to work hard to keep your temper. In most situations however, you should be able to remain calm.

2 SUNDAY   *Moon Age Day 22   Moon Sign Taurus*

Trends move on and today you can enjoy a fairly high profile, particularly in social situations. It looks as though you can shine like a star when the mood takes you but on the other hand, you can be fairly sulky and to react badly if you are prevailed upon to do anything that really goes against the grain.

3 MONDAY   *Moon Age Day 23   Moon Sign Gemini*

Some long-held dreams can be your goal now, as people move heaven and earth to make you happy. In particular, look out for favourable influences at work. This is a time during which your actions are being closely watched and it is likely that the opinions being made about you are favourable.

4 TUESDAY   *Moon Age Day 24   Moon Sign Gemini*

If your partner proves less agreeable than usual, maybe you should look for the reason within yourself. Have you forgotten an anniversary or some other important event? Have you been inconsiderate in any way? Make a few kind gestures but don't go overboard, as this can make matters worse.

5 WEDNESDAY   *Moon Age Day 25   Moon Sign Cancer*

Remember there is only so much you can control on your own. The more you are willing to co-operate today, the better things are likely to go for you. It doesn't matter how hard you try, in the eyes of a very few people everything you do is wrong. Simply try to ignore this and stick to people you find reasonable.

6 THURSDAY   *Moon Age Day 26   Moon Sign Cancer*

In personal encounters, your competitive nature is stimulated. There's no problem as long as your opposite number knows how to lose gracefully. It seems as though there are very few demands you would shy away from on this particular Thursday but do avoid taking on more than you can cope with.

7 FRIDAY   *Moon Age Day 27   Moon Sign Leo*

In this generally progressive phase, you have plenty of power at your fingertips on those occasions you need it the most. When it comes to forward planning, you are second to none. Give way to the ideas of your partner, or to someone you count as a really good and loyal friend, if you know it is important to them.

8 SATURDAY   *Moon Age Day 28   Moon Sign Leo*

The Sun in your solar seventh house is particularly helpful when it comes to one-to-one contacts but that doesn't mean you fail to be good in more social situations. The choice is definitely yours for the taking and the only thing that would really worry you is to be forced down roads you don't want to follow.

9 SUNDAY   *Moon Age Day 0   Moon Sign Virgo*

Progress is difficult now, mainly thanks to the lunar low. If you don't try to move mountains, you will not be upset when you find it impossible to do so. Concentrate on being quiet and doing things that please only you. Spending moments on your own is not difficult and may be the best course of action.

10 MONDAY
Moon Age Day 1   Moon Sign Virgo

Only attempt today what you really know is likely to work and stay clear of gambling or signing documents you don't really understand. If there are major purchases in the offing, try to leave them until tomorrow but if that proves to be impossible, check the details very carefully and maybe take a friend along for support.

11 TUESDAY
Moon Age Day 2   Moon Sign Libra

If you know you are telling the truth today, it is important to say that you are. This is necessary, even if you know you could upset someone else on the way. The problems will be much greater if you refuse to open your mouth now and could lead to some really harsh words further down the line.

12 WEDNESDAY
Moon Age Day 3   Moon Sign Libra

There are things happening in a career sense that you will probably enjoy a great deal. Getting on the right side of superiors should be quite easy because charm is your middle name at present. Don't go too far though, because the actions you take have to be believable to those you are trying to impress.

13 THURSDAY
Moon Age Day 4   Moon Sign Scorpio

Instinct and intuition guide you through a day that requires you to react at a moment's notice. The magnetic side of your Piscean nature is now fully on display and it is clear that you are out to impress in some way. Any element of tedium in your life right now is likely to be shunned instantly.

14 FRIDAY
Moon Age Day 5   Moon Sign Scorpio

A sense of emotional security is present today but you won't get away from the fact that general situations are changing rapidly and there is little you can do about it. Being quite creative at present, you may decide that the time is right for a new look and perhaps for buying some clothes that make others sit up and take notice.

15 SATURDAY   *Moon Age Day 6   Moon Sign Scorpio*

This is a Saturday during which you should have more time to please yourself. Rushing and pushing in amongst queues won't appeal to you at all, though walking along a deserted beach or looking down at the world from the top of a high hill probably will. You need to be anywhere that makes you feel free and alive.

16 SUNDAY   *Moon Age Day 7   Moon Sign Sagittarius*

There are influences around now that put you where the good times are. Don't be shy when it comes to showing what you are capable of doing and be willing to let your voice be heard. Although you might sometimes doubt your own abilities, in the end you are almost certain to come good.

17 MONDAY   *Moon Age Day 8   Moon Sign Sagittarius*

Things continue to go better and better on the one-to-one front. Friendship is also very important to you at this time and you won't have any trouble bringing your pals round to your way of thinking. Concern for the underdog is never very far from the surface as far as you are concerned and today is no exception.

18 TUESDAY   *Moon Age Day 9   Moon Sign Capricorn*

You have a real talent for communication and this fact is showing stronger than ever at the moment. Someone you haven't seen for a while is likely to pay a return visit to your life and could be bringing some surprises along with them. Getting to grips with a job you don't like will be quite tedious but still necessary.

19 WEDNESDAY   *Moon Age Day 10   Moon Sign Capricorn*

You have the capacity to be almost anything you would wish to be around now. Your confidence remains essentially high and there isn't much doubt about your desire to be the best in every situation. People gather round to ask your advice and what you are telling them might be at least partly appropriate for you too.

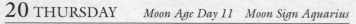

20 THURSDAY   *Moon Age Day 11   Moon Sign Aquarius*

Your social life now receives a definite boost. It is possible that you could be feeling most interested in superficial issues, if only because there isn't too much deep thinking going on. Don't worry, you manage to clock up enough hours plumbing the depths of your own Piscean nature and sometimes you really do need a lighter touch.

21 FRIDAY   *Moon Age Day 12   Moon Sign Aquarius*

You would be better off keeping all your options open today because there are not too many gains to be made by sticking to a specific point of view through thick and thin. In a few days the lunar high is with you and this would be an ideal time to clear the decks for a more positive sort of action.

22 SATURDAY   *Moon Age Day 13   Moon Sign Aquarius*

The Sun moves into your solar eighth house. During the next month or so you can expect the end of certain phases in your life and the commencement of new ones. This position of the Sun can also quite easily bring out the detective in you, making you need to know how everything works in minute detail.

23 SUNDAY   *Moon Age Day 14   Moon Sign Pisces*

The lunar high could easily bring a Sunday to remember. It seems you can be an expert at just about anything now and will get jobs done whilst others stand around and stare. When it comes to winning Brownie points, days don't come much better than this one. Your prestige will be going out through the roof.

24 MONDAY   *Moon Age Day 15   Moon Sign Pisces*

Good luck is behind your actions, leading to a potentially very powerful Monday. If you happen to be at work, put in that extra bit of effort that gets you noticed and which could make all the difference in the longer-term. On the other hand, if you can avoid work today, this would be a great time to go out and have fun.

25 TUESDAY *Moon Age Day 16   Moon Sign Aries*

The ordinary in life doesn't seem all that attractive to you at present, maybe because things have been so exciting of late. There are tedious jobs to be done but you either get them out of the way quickly or manage to find someone to do them for you. Pisces is definitely calling in a few favours at this stage of the week.

26 WEDNESDAY *Moon Age Day 17   Moon Sign Aries*

You can be very sympathetic to the needs of those around you at the best of times but this quality is specifically emphasised at present. Consideration and concern are now your middle names. This is particularly the case with regard to family members but friends will also be on the receiving end of your concern.

27 THURSDAY *Moon Age Day 18   Moon Sign Aries*

It may be time to do some serious thinking about a course of action you have taken recently. It isn't too late to modify your plans and there is no shame in doing so if you think it would suit your purposes better. Even if certain people accuse you of vacillating, what matters are your ultimate actions and successes.

28 FRIDAY *Moon Age Day 19   Moon Sign Taurus*

If you have to abandon something and start again, then so be it. What you shouldn't do is to carry on regardless, even when you know that you are going in the wrong direction. Friends will offer some timely advice but don't spend all day on practical matters because there is fun to be had later.

29 SATURDAY *Moon Age Day 20   Moon Sign Taurus*

The more variety you can get into your life right now, the better you are going to feel about it. Any uncertainty that has dogged you during the last few days is now likely to disappear and you will become far more certain of yourself and your actions. Keep in touch with people who are living at a distance or even abroad.

30 SUNDAY   *Moon Age Day 21   Moon Sign Gemini*

This is a very good time to socialise and to get onside with people who haven't always been your cup of tea in the past. Not everyone has the same ideas as you do and it will take time to explain your thoughts to those around you. Today has a leisurely quality that makes this process easier.

October

2018

1 MONDAY
Moon Age Day 22   Moon Sign Gemini

You are entering a pretty dynamic and competitive phase at work and Pisceans who are not in work at present should definitely be keeping their eyes open now. It isn't out of the question that some Pisceans will be taking a holiday around this time. If so, you have chosen wisely and should have an excellent break.

2 TUESDAY
Moon Age Day 23   Moon Sign Cancer

A personal matter is likely to put you on the defensive today but do make sure you are not defending yourself before you have even been attacked. The people who matter the most will be on your side at the moment and are unlikely to let you down, even if the going gets a little difficult.

3 WEDNESDAY
Moon Age Day 24   Moon Sign Cancer

This should be a potentially wonderful time in terms of personal relationships. There are quite a few planetary aspects and positions now working in your favour and very little to get in the way of romantic bliss. If you are not involved in a personal attachment right now, perhaps you should be keeping your eyes open.

4 THURSDAY
Moon Age Day 25   Moon Sign Leo

If you have to rethink a particular plan of action, don't see this as being necessary bad. On the contrary, the more you rush into things right now, the greater is the likelihood of making a mistake, so take plenty of time to organise things methodically. People you haven't seen for quite some time could be making a renewed appearance in your life today.

5 FRIDAY
Moon Age Day 26   Moon Sign Leo

This may be the best time of this month to have a clear out in your life. It could be that there are certain business or social relationships that have been holding you back or people who simply don't seem to have your best interests at heart. You are far from being hard-hearted but may be forced by circumstances to look again at situations.

6 SATURDAY
Moon Age Day 27   Moon Sign Virgo

This certainly isn't the most progressive day of the month. The lunar low can make you feel sluggish and could see you putting off something you have been planning for a while. Make the day your own by doing exactly what takes your fancy. If that means curling up with a book, then so be it.

7 SUNDAY
Moon Age Day 28   Moon Sign Virgo

Major decisions are left until later. You are not really in a position to take chances at the moment and might regret it if you do. For the moment, simply coast along and watch others setting the pace. You should be able to get a good deal from friendships and pastimes that you always enjoy so focus on these for now.

8 MONDAY
Moon Age Day 29   Moon Sign Virgo

Any outdoor pursuits you may follow are especially well highlighted now, as the more sporting and competitive side of your nature also beings to show itself. Because you are feeling brave at present, you may choose to tackle an issue that has had you quaking in your boots at some stage in the past.

9 TUESDAY
Moon Age Day 0   Moon Sign Libra

This may be the time to bring something to a successful conclusion – this inclination has been around in your chart for the last few days but it looks even more pertinent now. Be on the lookout for ways to improve your life and also your finances. A change of scene would probably be welcome.

10 WEDNESDAY   *Moon Age Day 1   Moon Sign Libra*

It can benefit you greatly to keep in touch with people who are in the know. Because of your generally affable ways, people like you a great deal. Turn this fact to your advantage for once and call in some assistance. Moving towards the culmination of plans you hatched some time ago, you make material progress.

11 THURSDAY   *Moon Age Day 2   Moon Sign Scorpio*

With a greater sense of freedom and adventure than you have experienced for some weeks, it looks as though this part of October is turning very much to your advantage. What you find within yourself right now is greater confidence and a desire to get on well, both practically and socially.

12 FRIDAY   *Moon Age Day 3   Moon Sign Scorpio*

Your potential for personal freedom is very strong. This can make you something of a loose cannon on occasions because people who think they know you well are likely to be constantly surprised by your actions and reactions. It doesn't do any harm at all to keep the world guessing once in a while.

13 SATURDAY   *Moon Age Day 4   Moon Sign Sagittarius*

Some emotional issues can seem to be more trouble than they are worth but it may be that a crucial issue between yourself and someone you love simply has to receive an airing at this time. Of course, you will be as tactful as always but you simply cannot leave things alone to possibly deteriorate further.

14 SUNDAY   *Moon Age Day 5   Moon Sign Sagittarius*

This is a marvellous period to get out into the world of social interaction and to make certain that your voice is heard. You will be making some new contacts this Sunday, most likely people who will become firm friends and who are in a good position to offer you some timely support.

15 MONDAY   *Moon Age Day 6   Moon Sign Capricorn*

Close, emotional involvement should now prove more satisfying than ever. This is not likely to be a quiet Monday but it does offer you the chance to show loved ones how important they are to you. Your sense of balance is good and you will instinctively know how and when to offer the best advice.

16 TUESDAY   *Moon Age Day 7   Moon Sign Capricorn*

You now decide to get down to the real nitty-gritty of life and you won't have any trouble at all convincing your family and friends that the decisions you make are the best ones in an all-round sense. Love is high on your agenda and you manage to find exactly the right words to please your partner now.

17 WEDNESDAY   *Moon Age Day 8   Moon Sign Capricorn*

Weigh up specific options carefully because it is entirely possible to make significant mistakes today if you rush into anything. Getting on side with someone who has proved to be difficult in the past should now be easier, mainly because your own frame of mind is very adaptable at present.

18 THURSDAY   *Moon Age Day 9   Moon Sign Aquarius*

Professionally speaking, you may decide that you cannot afford to miss out on anything today. Throw your efforts into opportunities at work, but not to the exclusion of all else. You should also be able to find plenty of diversion coming from the direction of friends, many of whom definitely have your best interests at heart.

19 FRIDAY   *Moon Age Day 10   Moon Sign Aquarius*

This would be a good time to join forces with friends or maybe neighbours in order to sort out something you are definitely not happy about. Pisces is a natural crusader, especially against unfairness of any sort. Outside of work you may find that you have far less time for personal enjoyment today than you might have wished.

20 SATURDAY
Moon Age Day 11   Moon Sign Pisces

This is a day of high energy and maximum achievement. Catapulted out of any twelfth house moon lethargy, you now surge forward positively, making for a potentially interesting and eventful weekend. Confusion of any sort is blown away by a necessary and welcome wind of change.

21 SUNDAY
Moon Age Day 12   Moon Sign Pisces

Getting your own way with others ought to be a piece of cake at the moment. With a natural sense of good luck, together with poise, balance and a determination to get on well, very little should be denied you this Sunday. The thing to avoid is staying around at home with nothing particular to do.

22 MONDAY
Moon Age Day 13   Moon Sign Pisces

Making any sort of important change is likely to be quite easy today, though you may have to deal with the slightly odd behaviour of a few of the people you are relying on at this time. Controversy is likely at some stage during the day, even if you are not the one who is inspiring it.

23 TUESDAY
Moon Age Day 14   Moon Sign Aries

You can get a great deal out of journeys of any sort and although the summer is now over, you might decide that the time is right to take a holiday. Travel that is organised at very short notice could be the most enjoyable of all and you can also gain from mixing with people who come from far away.

24 WEDNESDAY
Moon Age Day 15   Moon Sign Aries

Success right now has a great deal to do with the influence you have over others. You may have to change your mind about something you thought you understood well but you won't lose credibility if you are able to explain yourself. Controversy can still dog your footsteps, this time maybe in terms of your personal life.

25 THURSDAY
Moon Age Day 16   Moon Sign Taurus

Contact with a variety of different sorts of people really makes life go with a swing and you cannot afford to hide either your nature or your talents at present. If you are good at something, now is the time to show the fact to the world at large. Romance could be on the cards for both young and young-at-heart Pisceans.

26 FRIDAY
Moon Age Day 17   Moon Sign Taurus

A personal plan or a specific intention on your part may now have to be scrapped, probably through no fault of your own. If this leads to some disappointment, the best way forward is to forget about a situation that is in the past and to pull even harder for the winning post in other ways. People make a fuss of you later today.

27 SATURDAY
Moon Age Day 18   Moon Sign Gemini

You should let your personality shine out this weekend because there are plenty of people watching you, some of whom are deeply attracted to that Piscean nature of yours. Don't be too modest and when you are asked for your opinion, do your best to act as though you have the right to offer it.

28 SUNDAY
Moon Age Day 19   Moon Sign Gemini

Ideas could fail to turn out quite as you had expected and that could mean having to alter your strategy at a moment's notice. This shouldn't present you with too many problems, since your mind is working quickly and you don't have too much trouble thinking on your feet under present astrological trends.

29 MONDAY
Moon Age Day 20   Moon Sign Cancer

There are planets around now that emphasise your obligations to others, which might be something of a drag during one of those few occasions for Pisces that you are thinking about yourself. It won't be long before a particularly tedious job is out of the way, which should leave you with more time to do what you want.

30 TUESDAY — *Moon Age Day 21   Moon Sign Cancer*

Seek change and variety for its own sake today and don't allow yourself to be held to one spot or a particular way of thinking. There are some gains to be made, not least of all in terms of the way you are looking at romantic matters. However, don't get sucked into the crazy schemes of someone you already fear could be a control-freak.

31 WEDNESDAY — *Moon Age Day 22   Moon Sign Cancer*

Socially speaking, this should be a very beneficial period. Present influences can bring you into contact with people from many different walks of life. Your horizons will be broadened immensely and it looks as though you have extra energy when you need it the most. Best of all, romance shines brightly in your life.

November
2018

1 THURSDAY
Moon Age Day 23   Moon Sign Leo

The first day of November could represent a good time for some sort of professional accomplishment. Certain matters that have been on hold for a while could come to fruition now and the chance of making money is quite good. Friends may have special needs of you around this time.

2 FRIDAY
Moon Age Day 24   Moon Sign Leo

Social highlights are present in your chart, making this a very good time for having fun and for making new friends. There are a number of confidences coming your way right now and it is very important that you guard these carefully since your reputation with some might rest on your discretion.

3 SATURDAY
Moon Age Day 25   Moon Sign Virgo

You have really been pushing hard this week and such is your momentum that it will carry you well into the lunar low before you even recognise its presence. All the same, it might be advisable to ease off somewhat, particularly when it comes to taking unnecessary and perhaps slightly foolish chances.

4 SUNDAY
Moon Age Day 26   Moon Sign Virgo

If there is a problem around today, it could well be your over-emotional tendencies. You would be well advised to use practical common sense, rather than to allow your naturally kind ways to influence your judgement. Someone could be out to take you for a ride, but not if you pay attention to what they are doing.

5 MONDAY   *Moon Age Day 27   Moon Sign Libra*

This is a period during which you should be getting as much rest as possible. It isn't that any trends are working against your best interests but simply that you have reached the end of a particular phase and need to take a break before starting on something else. From a personal viewpoint, today should find you very content.

6 TUESDAY   *Moon Age Day 28   Moon Sign Libra*

There are some new and interesting people around at the moment. If you haven't already taken this fact into account, maybe you should do so today. Whether you meet these people at work, or within your home-life, you can get a great deal out of new encounters. These should furnish you with schemes and plans for next year.

7 WEDNESDAY   *Moon Age Day 0   Moon Sign Scorpio*

You can make today very interesting for yourself but there are a few small setbacks to take into account. It is possible that in the middle of enjoying yourself, there will be a number of people around who have it in mind that you should be working. If you become aware of this you are likely to feel it is an injustice – and even Pisces fights back sometimes.

8 THURSDAY   *Moon Age Day 1   Moon Sign Scorpio*

You are out there in the social mainstream today, even if that is not exactly where you planned on being. On every level, work takes something of a back seat in favour of having fun for a little while. Your confidence is far from lacking, especially when you are in the company of people who naturally make you feel good.

9 FRIDAY   *Moon Age Day 2   Moon Sign Sagittarius*

You are still in a go-ahead frame of mind but you manifest this slightly differently now. If someone is needed to cheer up a really sad individual, then that person is definitely you. Your sense of humour is especially infectious and you have a natural wisdom that hardly anyone could fail to recognise.

143

10 SATURDAY   *Moon Age Day 3   Moon Sign Sagittarius*

You feel the need to broaden your horizons as much as possible today, so avoid being in any way restricted in your thinking. Pisces is full of very creative ideas around now, a factor that can stand you in good stead, both at home and work. Keep abreast of current affairs to broaden your mind, too.

11 SUNDAY   *Moon Age Day 4   Moon Sign Sagittarius*

The opportunities for overall gain are good today, though you could find yourself so keen on breaking down barriers and achieving more personal freedom that you don't address the financial aspect of life at all. Avoid listening to either rumours or gossip, both of which are likely to give you false information.

12 MONDAY   *Moon Age Day 5   Moon Sign Capricorn*

This is a good day from a professional point of view and it is easy to make allies at every stage. A continued reliance on a certain individual could lead to one or two problems, especially if the person concerned fails to live up to your expectations. Embark on new projects with as much confidence as you can muster.

13 TUESDAY   *Moon Age Day 6   Moon Sign Capricorn*

Contacts with superiors at work might lead to a better understanding and could even prove advantageous to you personally in the fullness of time. A task to which there seems to have been no end should be drawing to a close before very long, leaving you with more time to do other things.

14 WEDNESDAY   *Moon Age Day 7   Moon Sign Aquarius*

Don't expect life to organise itself, particularly at work. You may have to pitch in early in the day, possibly to sort out a mess made by someone else. With good humour and the understanding that is born into Pisces people, you attend to things today and maintain a happy frame of mind.

15 THURSDAY   *Moon Age Day 8   Moon Sign Aquarius*

It is easier to address the needs and wants of loved ones today, rather than spending too much time thinking about what you want for yourself. This is the truly unselfish quality of Pisces, which is never really very far from the surface. Your intuition works well when you are dealing with strangers.

16 FRIDAY   *Moon Age Day 9   Moon Sign Aquarius*

Current trends leave you with some new directions to travel, either in a real or a figurative sense. You might not be feeling particularly brave at present but this doesn't show and just about everyone you meet is impressed with you. Don't be too quick to step aside in favour of someone else if there is something you really want.

17 SATURDAY   ☿   *Moon Age Day 10   Moon Sign Pisces*

The Moon returns to your sign and brings with it what is potentially the most outgoing and fun-loving period of the month. You articulate your needs and wants particularly well and know how to make it possible for those around you to have an especially good and enjoyable time. Enjoy the buzz.

18 SUNDAY   ☿   *Moon Age Day 11   Moon Sign Pisces*

This is the high point in maintaining the sort of progress more normally associated with the Fire-signs in the zodiac, such as Aries. Although you fortunately fail to manifest the more selfish aspects of some of your more gregarious zodiac cousins, you certainly know how to paint the town red at the moment.

19 MONDAY   ☿   *Moon Age Day 12   Moon Sign Aries*

You should prepare yourself for some heart-warming surprises and for a few gains that you didn't expect. Everyday matters bring the results you have been expecting and probably more besides. With a positive and useful week ahead, you may decide to start enjoying yourself long before today is over.

20 TUESDAY ☿ *Moon Age Day 13   Moon Sign Aries*

You will be attending to a number of different jobs today but like the juggler you are it is possible to keep all the balls in the air at the same time. Not everyone believes in you right now but the people who matter the most will and that fact is enough to see you through one or two potentially sticky moments.

21 WEDNESDAY ☿ *Moon Age Day 14   Moon Sign Taurus*

You should find yourself on the right side of some interesting situations today, even if you have to dream them up for yourself. Not everyone displays the same sort of sense of humour that you do right now but that doesn't matter because you will make them laugh in one way or another. Look after cash in the afternoon and evening.

22 THURSDAY ☿ *Moon Age Day 15   Moon Sign Taurus*

A boost to teamwork and all co-operative ventures comes along at this time and you should make the most of these positive trends. You are getting on well with just about everyone, even if there are one or two awkward types around. Your creative potential is especially good and some Pisceans will be thinking about redecorating.

23 FRIDAY ☿ *Moon Age Day 16   Moon Sign Taurus*

When it comes to furthering your ambitions you are clearly second to none, even though you might have to enlist the support of others on the way. There are likely to be some unexpected events around this time but you should manage to deal with them relatively easily. If you are currently single, there is a chance you could start a new relationship now.

24 SATURDAY ☿ *Moon Age Day 17   Moon Sign Gemini*

Close companions may now cause you to think quite deeply about the importance you have placed upon relationships of late. It is possible that you may decide to spend some of your social hours with people you don't see very often. This would be a good day for sending letters or for making a long-distance telephone call.

25 SUNDAY ☿ *Moon Age Day 18* *Moon Sign Gemini*

New life may now be breathed into situations you thought were over and done with. Expect friends to take you into their confidence, and make sure you understand the importance of keeping it. Friends are likely to be particularly demanding of your time and that won't leave quite as many hours as you might have wished for practical matters.

26 MONDAY ☿ *Moon Age Day 19* *Moon Sign Cancer*

Self-confidence in professional matters is clearly the way forward and you won't get anywhere at all if you fail to show those around you that you know what you are talking about. In social and family situations you are putting everyone ahead of yourself, which isn't exactly unusual for Pisces.

27 TUESDAY ☿ *Moon Age Day 20* *Moon Sign Cancer*

There may be a number of advantages for you in assuming a high profile in connection with your professional life. It doesn't matter how lowly you consider your position at work to be, you now have the ability to make it really count. For some Pisceans, there are new responsibilities on offer.

28 WEDNESDAY ☿ *Moon Age Day 21* *Moon Sign Leo*

Long-term ambitions and major aims are likely to be within easier reach at this stage. Your future is now more definitely in your own hands than seems to have been the case for a while. The middle of the working week may also bring you to a specific decision that has been pending for ages. Friends should prove helpful now.

29 THURSDAY ☿ *Moon Age Day 22* *Moon Sign Leo*

Your intuition is now much increased and you need to turn it in the direction of people who are coming new into your life. These might be individuals who you meet professionally, or perhaps potential friends for the future. Not everything is what it seems – and you have what it takes to work out why.

30 FRIDAY
☿ *Moon Age Day 23   Moon Sign Virgo*

You now have to put up with the lunar low, though for a host of astrological reasons you might fail to even notice its presence now. The fact is that you have great momentum and can shoot through difficult moments without registering them. You do have to watch out for the odd conman though, because not everyone is trustworthy.

December 2018

1 SATURDAY   ☿   *Moon Age Day 24*   *Moon Sign Virgo*

A lack of progress could annoy you today although there is a good chance that you won't lose too much momentum, or else you are not really seeking any. Some Pisceans will be slowing down a little now, and as it is the weekend you can indulge any desire to enjoy yourself without any sense of guilt.

2 SUNDAY   ☿   *Moon Age Day 25*   *Moon Sign Libra*

The things that are the most enjoyable now are to be found out there in the wider world. With plenty to play for and more than a modicum of good luck on your side, you can afford to back your hunches. People you haven't seen for some time could soon be in touch and correspondence generally proves important.

3 MONDAY   ☿   *Moon Age Day 26*   *Moon Sign Libra*

The things you learn from colleagues today can be of supreme importance, so you must pay attention to what is said around you. Pisceans who are looking for work or a change of employment could also be in luck around this time. When it comes to out-of-work activities, new interests take your fancy.

4 TUESDAY   ☿   *Moon Age Day 27*   *Moon Sign Scorpio*

The ideas that others have will not be exactly to your liking now and you are much more likely to focus on your own schemes and plans. Whether or not you can bring important people round to your way of thinking remains to be seen. There are some quite significant changes up ahead for some Pisceans.

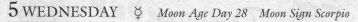

5 WEDNESDAY ☿ *Moon Age Day 28   Moon Sign Scorpio*

It is now the more practical aspects of life that appeal to you the most. In the main, you will want to do your own thing today and won't take kindly to being bossed around by anyone. The end of a particular phase in your life is not too far away and although it will bring the odd sigh of nostalgia, the gains outweigh the losses.

6 THURSDAY ☿ *Moon Age Day 29   Moon Sign Scorpio*

You should enjoy being on the move as much as possible but don't allow distractions to get in the way of real financial success. Dragging yourself back to practicalities might not seem all that inspiring but could prove to be quite important all the same. It is also a good time to begin making plans for Christmas.

7 FRIDAY *Moon Age Day 0   Moon Sign Sagittarius*

Don't dither or hang back when it comes to making major decisions. The more ambitious you are, the greater is the potential for success. Results you have been seeking for some time will be closer than you think and you have tremendous potential for doing just the right thing when it matters the most.

8 SATURDAY *Moon Age Day 1   Moon Sign Sagittarius*

The planetary emphasis falls on finances, probably not surprising at this expensive time of the year. You are quite canny at the moment and know full well how to get value for money. Look around because there could be one or two things available for Christmas that you can get at rock-bottom prices.

9 SUNDAY *Moon Age Day 2   Moon Sign Capricorn*

A possible mistake you might make today is to take on too many diverse interests. You would be much better off concentrating on one thing at a time and therefore avoiding unnecessary mistakes. Methodical actions may lead to success, but there will still be plenty of time in which to enjoy yourself.

10 MONDAY   *Moon Age Day 3   Moon Sign Capricorn*

A fast pace of events in the professional or practical world is probably what you can expect today. There is vital information there for the taking and you won't be slow to pick up on what others are trying to tell you. Give yourself a pat on the back for a recent personal success but don't allow it to go to your head.

11 TUESDAY   *Moon Age Day 4   Moon Sign Aquarius*

Faces old and new come along now ahead of the Christmas period. You might be deliberately taking a trip down memory lane at some stage today because that is what Christmas is all about. With less than two weeks to go, most Pisceans should now be pleased with the arrangements they have made for the holidays.

12 WEDNESDAY   *Moon Age Day 5   Moon Sign Aquarius*

A continuing improvement in a general sense makes itself felt most in terms of work and your ability to attract money. Your decision-making is good at present and you can afford to back your hunches to a greater extent. Friends should prove to be quite reliable and there are some new pals in the offing.

13 THURSDAY   *Moon Age Day 6   Moon Sign Aquarius*

A sense of variety and freedom is both important and appealing to Pisceans at this time. Don't be a stick-in-the-mud. Although this might not be exactly the season for outdoor activities, you might find the lure of the wild appealing. Later in the day, you might choose to spend at least some time alone.

14 FRIDAY   *Moon Age Day 7   Moon Sign Pisces*

Getting into heated debates could be more enjoyable than you might imagine and with the lunar high now present, you are hardly likely to lose. Back your hunches to the hilt and do what you can to make progress your middle name. There isn't too much time before the holidays, so make the best of what is available.

15 SATURDAY
Moon Age Day 8   Moon Sign Pisces

Your potential for lucky breaks is greater than usual and you won't be inclined to look on the dark side of any situation at present. Getting favours from others proves to be especially easy and your general level of popularity seems higher than ever. In reality, you are always popular but you realise it more at this time.

16 SUNDAY
Moon Age Day 9   Moon Sign Pisces

The quickening pace around you in everyday life now shows at every turn and you will barely have time to breathe right now. Don't leave travel plans to chance but make sure that all details are sorted well in advance. This might be a journey you intend to take this week or perhaps even as late as Christmas or New Year.

17 MONDAY
Moon Age Day 10   Moon Sign Aries

A boost to all social matters comes along and it looks as though you are already well into a Christmas frame of mind. All is happiness around you and if you have been a little restricted by the negative attitude of friends or family members, this sort of situation is now likely to be disappearing.

18 TUESDAY
Moon Age Day 11   Moon Sign Aries

Intellectual inspiration comes your way via travel and social discussions. It seems that others find you extremely entertaining to have around and they could be making you feel almost like a celebrity at the moment. Expect friends to share confidences with you, even some friends who are not usually forthcoming with their problems.

19 WEDNESDAY
Moon Age Day 12   Moon Sign Taurus

Some people might describe you as being too assertive at present but if they do it's probably only because they are used to getting their own way. All that is happening is that you know what you want from life and are presently willing to say so. Avoid getting into pointless discussions about things that don't matter.

20 THURSDAY   *Moon Age Day 13   Moon Sign Taurus*

You can capitalise on new opportunities today and won't be stuck when it comes to expressing your opinions, no matter who is on the receiving end. Although you might not have too much professional influence for today, there are ideas coming into your mind at the moment that you will act upon before long.

21 FRIDAY   *Moon Age Day 14   Moon Sign Gemini*

You are presently filled with a definite urge to work hard and to get what you want from life. Not everyone is in the same frame of mind as you are and there isn't much doubt that people's general holiday spirit is getting in your way at a time when you are in a practical mood. Some Piscean patience is called for.

22 SATURDAY   *Moon Age Day 15   Moon Sign Gemini*

This can be an especially rewarding day for many Pisceans, a situation that is brought about as a result of a cocktail of positive planetary positions. You may be able to confirm one or two suspicions regarding someone you haven't trusted for a while but in the main you find others to be reliable and helpful.

23 SUNDAY   *Moon Age Day 16   Moon Sign Cancer*

This would be a good time to take a short break and to mull over your present successes. Of course you won't be able to see everything in its true light just at the moment but where it matters the most you begin to see some light at the end of the tunnel. Friends will demand your time but you will help if you can.

24 MONDAY   *Moon Age Day 17   Moon Sign Cancer*

Christmas Eve is likely to see an increase in general progress, followed by a lull that comes later in the day. Routines will be tedious, though it won't be long before the excitement of the day takes over. Family members are the source of much joy and you should be happily looking forward to tomorrow.

25 TUESDAY
Moon Age Day 18   Moon Sign Leo

Although you may feel a need to get out of doors to soak up the Christmas spirit, this won't stop you from having a particularly good and enjoyable day. Travel is most likely to come very soon but for the moment, enjoy feeling warm, secure and surrounded by love in the bosom of your family.

26 WEDNESDAY
Moon Age Day 19   Moon Sign Leo

Positive influences surround social gatherings, which probably makes Boxing Day the most potentially riotous and enjoyable day of the holidays. You are less inclined to seek your own surroundings now, so perhaps you are deciding to go on a family visit. Routine jobs should definitely be put on hold at present.

27 THURSDAY
Moon Age Day 20   Moon Sign Virgo

Some of the things that are happening around you now seem less fulfilling. You need to broaden your horizons somewhat and should not be intimidated by little setbacks. The lunar low doesn't really help the situation but whether or not you enjoy what today has on offer seems to be up to you.

28 FRIDAY
Moon Age Day 21   Moon Sign Virgo

Although you are in the middle of a planetary lull, you can still make the most of today. Let others make the running and simply turn up to have a good time. At least part of today will be spent deliberately alone, perhaps thinking about the year that lies ahead. A more positive attitude comes along by the evening.

29 SATURDAY
Moon Age Day 22   Moon Sign Libra

Right now you should be enjoying high points in love and romantic affairs, not to mention a definite boost to your ego that comes from a number of different directions. You clearly believe in yourself and while this is the case you won't be short of ideas or ways in which you can make them work out as you would wish.

30 SUNDAY   *Moon Age Day 23   Moon Sign Libra*

Stand by for a fairly brisk time socially and you will almost certainly find that some of the recent frustrations are now disappearing. Your confidence is strong but you are willing to suspend some actions until next week. As a result there is more time available to simply enjoy yourself in the company of family and friends.

31 MONDAY   *Moon Age Day 24   Moon Sign Libra*

It is just possible that your love life might unfortunately prove to be slightly problematic on this New Year's Even. Although this reminds you that you have to show that extra bit of concern and love, take heart from the fact that it shouldn't be a lasting situation. If you open your eyes to the needs of those around you, it is possible to have everything fully on course for a splendid evening.

RISING SIGNS FOR PISCES

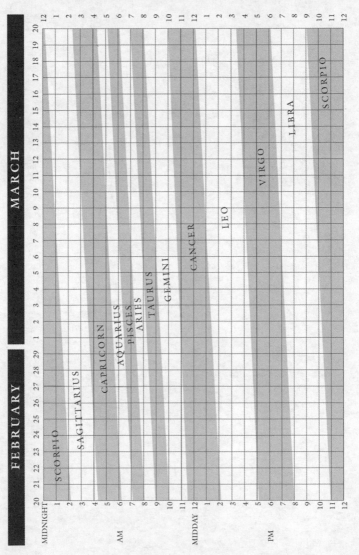

THE ZODIAC, PLANETS
AND CORRESPONDENCES

The Earth revolves around the Sun once every calendar year, so when viewed from Earth the Sun appears in a different part of the sky as the year progresses. In astrology, these parts of the sky are divided into the signs of the zodiac and this means that the signs are organised in a circle. The circle begins with Aries and ends with Pisces.

Taking the zodiac sign as a starting point, astrologers then work with all the positions of planets, stars and many other factors to calculate horoscopes and birth charts and tell us what the stars have in store for us.

The table below shows the planets and Elements for each of the signs of the zodiac. Each sign belongs to one of the four Elements: Fire, Air, Earth or Water. Fire signs are creative and enthusiastic; Air signs are mentally active and thoughtful; Earth signs are constructive and practical; Water signs are emotional and have strong feelings.

It also shows the metals and gemstones associated with, or corresponding with, each sign. The correspondence is made when a metal or stone possesses properties that are held in common with a particular sign of the zodiac.

Finally, the table shows the opposite of each star sign – this is the opposite sign in the astrological circle.

Placed	Sign	Symbol	Element	Planet	Metal	Stone	Opposite
1	Aries	Ram	Fire	Mars	Iron	Bloodstone	Libra
2	Taurus	Bull	Earth	Venus	Copper	Sapphire	Scorpio
3	Gemini	Twins	Air	Mercury	Mercury	Tiger's Eye	Sagittarius
4	Cancer	Crab	Water	Moon	Silver	Pearl	Capricorn
5	Leo	Lion	Fire	Sun	Gold	Ruby	Aquarius
6	Virgo	Maiden	Earth	Mercury	Mercury	Sardonyx	Pisces
7	Libra	Scales	Air	Venus	Copper	Sapphire	Aries
8	Scorpio	Scorpion	Water	Pluto	Plutonium	Jasper	Taurus
9	Sagittarius	Archer	Fire	Jupiter	Tin	Topaz	Gemini
10	Capricorn	Goat	Earth	Saturn	Lead	Black Onyx	Cancer
11	Aquarius	Waterbearer	Air	Uranus	Uranium	Amethyst	Leo
12	Pisces	Fishes	Water	Neptune	Tin	Moonstone	Virgo